Part I Useful T
- Chapter 1 Paying 4
- Chapter 2 Common Myths & Misconceptions & Mistakes 11
- Chapter 3 Using this Guide 14

Part II The Fundamentals of Financial Aid
- Chapter 4 Definitions & Players 16
- Chapter 5 This You Must Understand 20
- Chapter 6 Taking Charge of the Link-Up Process 22

Part III Advanced Moves in Financial Aid
- Chapter 7 For the Short-Range: Tilting Things Your Way 34
- Chapter 8 Long Range Planning: College is Still Years Away 44

Part IV The Major Money Sources
- Chapter 9 The Colleges 50
- Chapter 10 Uncle Sam 58
- Chapter 11 The States 65

Part V The Big Alternatives
- Chapter 12 Letting the Boss Pay for It 72
- Chapter 13 Putting On the Uniform. 74

Part VI Special Opportunities
- Chapter 14 Private Sources with Few Strings 80
- Chapter 15 Money in Your Community 81
- Chapter 16 Are Your Parents Eligible? 83
- Chapter 17 Money From Your Affiliations 85
- Chapter 18 Money Because You Have Brains and Talent 88
- Chapter 19 Money Because You are an Athlete 92
- Chapter 20 Money for Health Careers 94
- Chapter 21 Money for Other Career Interests 99
- Chapter 22 Money for Women and Minorities 103
- Chapter 23 Special Situations: The Non-Traditional Student 107
- Chapter 24 A Few Words About Graduate School 109
- Chapter 25 A Treasure Chest of Tips 113

Appendices 115

Cover Design by Supon Design
Typesetting by Edington-Rand

© Copyright 1991 by Anna Leider

All rights reserved.

No part of this book may be reproduced in any form, by photostat, microfilm, xerography, or any other means, or incorporated into any information retrieval system, electronic or mechanical, without the written permission of the copyright owner. Violations of this provision will be vigorously prosecuted.

Care and diligence have been taken in organizing and presenting the data contained in *Don't Miss Out,* however, Octameron does not guarantee its accuracy. This edition contains information relevant to the 1992/93 academic year. The next edition will be available in September, 1992.

Address editorial correspondence to:
Octameron Associates, Inc.
P.O. Box 2748
Alexandria, VA 22301
(703) 836-5480

Address bookstore inquiries regarding purchases and returns to:
Dearborn Trade
520 N. Dearborn Street
Chicago, IL 60610
Outside Illinois, 800/245-BOOK
In Illinois, 800/836-4400 x270

ISBN 0-945981-48-1
PRINTED IN THE UNITED STATES OF AMERICA

Part I
Useful Things to Know

Chapter 1
Paying for College in the 90s

IT TAKES SPECIAL KNOWLEDGE
A college education is expensive. For some families it can be the largest expenditure they will ever make—more costly than the purchase of a house and with fewer years to make the payments.

Even though this may not be what you want to hear, don't throw up your hands and walk away from college. Financial help is available—plenty of it. But there is more to getting aid than matching up a list of addresses to a pile of stationary and a supply of stamps. It takes special knowledge. For instance:

Knowing Who Gets the Aid. The theory of student aid holds that assistance should go to those who need it the most. In practice, assistance is more likely to find its way to those who know how to apply, when to apply and where to apply. By understanding the application process—by taking charge, you have an advantage over those who enter the process in a passive mode. That advantage translates into a greater chance of receiving aid, larger awards, and more desirable awards in terms of their composition (in other words, awards that do not have to be paid back).

Knowing About The Buyer's Market. Students are a scarce commodity. Competition for them is intense. This competition creates opportunities—opportunities that you should maximize.

Knowing Basic Personal Finance Techniques. There are investments, gifts, low-interest loans, stripped bonds, and special lines of credit. When properly used, these schemes can be harnessed to student aid and reinforce its availability. When improperly used, they will cancel your eligibility for aid. You want to achieve the former and prevent the latter.

Knowing How to Tell Good Advice From Bad Advice. Advice on paying for college is plentiful. But not all of it is good. Some is dated. Some is wrong. And some is tainted by the self-interest of those who offer it.

Special knowledge is what this guide is all about. **Don't Miss Out** will teach you and your family how to formulate your own financial aid strategy—one that will lead you to a good, affordable higher education.

LOOKING FOR COLLEGE MONEY IS A FAMILY AFFAIR
A high school student told a newspaper reporter, "To ignore what your parents have to spend today, you've either got to be very thoughtless or very wealthy."

Well, you're not thoughtless, and you're not wealthy. That's why you're reading this book. Our advice to you: Read it not once, but twice—quickly the first time, to get the gist of the whole process; then slowly, taking notes on the college money options that best fit your family's situation.

After that, pass the book on to your parents. Why? Because paying for college is a family affair. You can't say, "Let them worry about it." They shouldn't say, "It's your problem." Everyone must be involved. The process must be well understood and the search must be started early. If these conditions aren't met, two things can and will happen. At best, the family will end up paying more for college than it should, or can afford. At worst, you will make a frantic, unplanned, last-minute college choice that is not in your best interest.

THE BIG PICTURE
The good news is that in 1992/93 approximately $34.5 billion in student aid will be available. Another bit of good news is that even more money is out there to be had. Uncle Sam's biggest

student aid effort, the Stafford Student Loan (formerly known as the Guaranteed Student Loan), is an entitlement program. That means everyone who is eligible for a loan can get a loan. But it takes an application. As the great Confucius would have said: Apply forget—no loan you get. Experts have guessed that several billions more could be tapped if the participation rate of eligibles jumped to 100%. Of course, if that were to occur, Uncle Sam would try to rebuild the program with a smaller entrance door.

The good news is balanced, as always, with bad news. Student expenses (and that includes tuition, room, board, books, fees, transportation, and miscellaneous costs) will total $87.8 billion. A second item of bad news is that student expenses, in the years to follow, will continue to take huge annual jumps while student aid will level off or even decline.

Take a good look at **Pie Charts A and B**. Note that Uncle Sam, the Colleges, the States, and Employer-Paid plans are the main sources of student aid. Not private scholarships. Our advice: When you decide where to look first, head for the table with the biggest plates. Don't crawl under the table looking for crumbs. Unfortunately, many student aid seekers don't follow this advice. They make the search for crumbs—that one percent of the Student Aid pie which represents private scholarships—their number one, and only priority. NOT SMART!

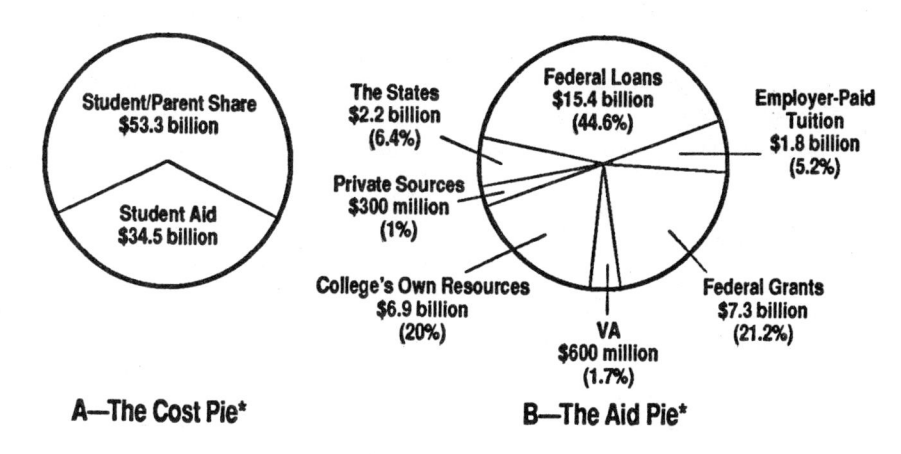

A—The Cost Pie*

- Student/Parent Share $53.3 billion
- Student Aid $34.5 billion

B—The Aid Pie*

- Federal Loans $15.4 billion (44.6%)
- The States $2.2 billion (6.4%)
- Private Sources $300 million (1%)
- College's Own Resources $6.9 billion (20%)
- VA $600 million (1.7%)
- Federal Grants $7.3 billion (21.2%)
- Employer-Paid Tuition $1.8 billion (5.2%)

Notes to Pie Chart B

Federal Loans include the Stafford and PLUS/SLS programs, Perkins revolving fund, HEAL and other health professions loans.

Employer-paid Tuition includes federal and private cooperative education programs.

Federal Grants include Pell, SEOG, SSIG, CW-S, Paul Douglas Teacher Scholarships, Robert Byrd Honors Scholarships, ROTC, military educational bonuses, military academies, health profession programs, various graduate programs, the Harry S. Truman Scholarship Foundation, and numerous smaller programs.

Veteran's Administration includes the GI Bill, VEAP, and various educational benefits to dependents of veterans.

College Resources include scholarships, the collegiate share of CW-S, non-subsidized student employment programs, short- and long-term loans from the colleges' own resources, and tuition remissions.

The States include the state share of federal programs, state grant programs and special loan programs that supplement Stafford and PLUS/SLS.

Other categories are self-explanatory.

*Figures are all estimated based on FY92 Budget requests.

LOOKING TO THE FUTURE

Our next point. Paying for college isn't a one-year, one-shot deal. You must think in terms of this year's costs, next year's costs, and the following year's costs. If tuition charges strain you now, how desperate are you going to be by the time you are a Junior? Or four years from now when you'll be a Senior, and graduating? You must have a sense of all the external factors that can come into play, those that assist you in your effort to meet educational expenses, as well as those that impede you.

How far out should your crystal ball extend? Four years, if you plan on a baccalaureate. Six years or more, if a graduate or professional degree is your objective. Ten years or more, if yours is a family with several college-bound students.

A lot will happen during the next four, six, or ten years. Some of it is uncertain, but a few trends stand out. You should be conscious of these trends and make them part of your continuous, long-range planning. Here are the most important ones:

TREND A: COLLEGE COSTS TO INCREASE FASTER THAN INFLATION

No sunshine here. But it's a hard fact and must be considered. Why do tuition hikes continue to outpace inflation?

- **Higher education is labor intensive.** For this reason, technological gain does not have as great an impact on "productivity" in the academic world as it does in the industrial world. Great teaching, as Socrates and Plato knew, comes from conversation between two inquiring minds. College students cannot be turned out like Model Ts. More teachers are needed.

   Within this larger trend, there are some smaller ones that bear close watching. For instance, in certain fields, such as engineering, computer science and geology, industry provides much higher salary scales than college departments. In consequence, graduate students are turning to industry and not to teaching, and professors now teaching are moving in increasing numbers from campus to corporate suites. To fight this trend, colleges must offer much more attractive salary packages. Meanwhile, the faculty shortages in these popular areas result in tougher admission standards for students seeking to major in these fields, more crowded classrooms, and less individualized attention.

- **State support of higher education is lagging behind costs.** The nation's public universities depend on state appropriations for 60% or more of their support. When state appropriations cannot keep pace with rising costs, the universities and community colleges must compensate by raising in-state tuitions and sky-rocketing their out-of-state charges (it's okay to slip it to out-of-staters: they vote somewhere else).

- **Computermania.** College after college is grabbing headlines by announcing that every student will be equipped with a personal computer. These computers must be linked by networks and supported by main frames. They need wiring, cooling, programming, maintenance people, a training staff, and what have you. All this costs money.

- **Technology.** If colleges are to be on the leading edge of technology, they must have the latest in laboratories, research equipment, machinery. Most of them don't have it now. Getting it will cost billions.

- **Deferred maintenance.** Leaky roofs. Crumbly foundations. Cracking asphalt. Inaccessible pipes. Paint jobs. Ivy won't hold up the walls forever. Recent estimates show our campuses need over $70 billion in repairs.

- **Fuel costs.** These are, proportionally, a far greater burden on college budgets than on family budgets. Old buildings, drafty halls, and a student population that overloads the circuits with electric gadgets ranging from hair dryers to popcorn poppers to VCRs to home computers keep the meters spinning.

- **The Robin Hood syndrome.** Collegiate student aid budgets, with very few exceptions, can no longer meet the financial need of all students. The common solution: Raise tuition charges through the roof; those who can pay will then, in effect, subsidize those who can't. Along these same lines, undergraduate tuition often subsidizes the education of graduate students, especially in the social sciences and humanities where grant money is increasingly scarce.

- **The declining prime age student population.** Each year the number of people reaching college age is declining. While some colleges have been able to make up the difference by enrolling increasing numbers of non-traditional students, others have not. At these less fortunate schools, fixed costs—plant, maintenance, tenured faculty salaries—are spread among fewer paying customers. To remain solvent, each student is asked to contribute more through higher tuitions.

- **Availability of federal student aid.** Some argue that the availability of federal student aid enables colleges to raise their price freely without suffering the consequence of decreased demand which makes overgenerous members of Congress partially responsible for increasing tuitions. Their reasoning uses simple principles of supply and demand. Every time colleges raise their price, constituents pressure Congress to appropriate more student aid. When student aid increases, colleges can again increase raise their tuition. Facts don't bear out this argument, however, it has received considerable attention and deserves some consideration as a legitimate factor.
- **Increased administration costs.** Red tape is rapidly encircling the nation's colleges and universities. Assistant and Associate Deans are everywhere, providing academic support, institutional support, and student services. College officials say these personnel costs are necessary and result from the need to administer many new student services and respond to increasingly complex, state and federal education regulations. But when you look at the numbers—a 61% increase in support staff over a ten-year period, as compared to a 5.9% increase in full-time faculty members during the same period—more schools might follow the example of Lehigh, Middlebury, Dartmouth, and San Diego State, all of which have eliminated dozens of jobs and millions of dollars from their administrative budgets. Welcome to the real world!
- **Price vs. quality.** While many people are growing uneasy over rising tuition costs, some of the nation's most competitive colleges have found the reverse to be true. These schools feel that many people judge quality by price; the greater the price tag, the higher the perceived quality, and the greater the applicant pool. Admission reports bear out this belief. Accordingly, some schools seem to raise their tuition at the same rate as their competitors regardless of projected budgets. In fact, it has been "suggested" that these colleges exchange information about their upcoming tuition increases and are now under investigation (see below).
- **Price fixing.** For the past 35 years, many of the nation's most prestigious schools had met each spring to share information about the amount of aid they would offer to their common (overlapping) applicants. Their goal was to come to an agreement about the abilities of these students to pay tuition bills. The schools felt this exchange was in the best interest of all involved. It allowed students to select a college based on academic needs and educational quality rather than economics. It also prevented bidding wars, which in turn, preserved financial aid funds for truly needy students. Families, however, saw it differently. In their eyes, this process denied them all the aid to which they were entitled. More importantly, it assumed they were unable to make decisions about what is and is not important to them in selecting a college. If price is a factor in that decision, then it's the family's right to have a choice of aid packages.

    Does this all sound like price fixing? For two years, the Justice Department investigated possible anti-trust violations (including the possiblility of collusion over tuition increases and the setting of faculty salaries) and as a result, the Ivies have now signed a consent decree to stop sharing information on student financial aid. Investigations continue against at least 15 other private institutions. While none of these schools (including the Ivies) admit to any collusion, the threat of a lengthy (and costly) court battle with the Justice Department, has effectively put the "Overlap Group" out of business.
- **Comparison shopping.** Fact. Colleges must compete for students. As students and parents become more sophisticated shoppers, they expect more for their money. Colleges must provide ample sports and recreational facilities for both men and women. They must maintain adequate levels of campus security, health care facilities (complete with resident psychologists, psychiatrists and drug/alcohol abuse counselors), and extensive career placement offices. Rooms must be wired for computers, hair driers and stereos. And dining halls must accommodate a variety of dietary requirements. As some of the above paragraphs point out, all of this costs money. The irony is, that the very people who complain about rising college costs are in part responsible for urging tuitions upward.
- **College is not as expensive as most people think.** Actually, we have a bit of good news. In a recent Gallop Poll, students placed the average cost (tuition and fees) of a private four-

year institution at $10,843 and the average cost of a public four-year institution at $6,841. These figures were substantially higher than actual tuition which at that time was $7,693 and $1,977 respectively. Adding in room and board brought the average costs up to $12,924 and $5,823. When you think about it, even today, with the cost of a private college averaging nearly $16,500, students are getting a pretty good deal. For what amounts to $75/day, the student is provided with a room (including heat, water and electricity), 3 meals a day, professional health care, recreational facilities, a wide range of social and cultural activities, counseling services, career assistance, and an education...

TREND B: YOUR FICKLE UNCLE SAM

Uncle Sam is the main dispenser of student aid. But Uncle changes his programs every year; sometimes, twice a year. His programs expand and shrink in dollar volume. Money that is authorized may never be appropriated. Money that is appropriated, can be rescinded. Eligibility for the programs is as variable as the dollars. In year A you may be eligible. In year B you are out. In year C you are in again—but for a different amount of aid.

This instability is not limited to dollars. It also extends to their delivery. Forms may be late. Deep questions must be resolved on such matters as how to verify selective service registration. The academic year may have started, the dollars appropriated, but the machinery for delivering the dollars is still being tuned.

To complicate matters, the United States faces a $277 billion dollar budget deficit. This impacts on the states' use of tax-exempt bonds to raise money to lend out to students, as Uncle needs all the tax dollars he can get. It has motivated Congress to pass tax reforms that eliminate many personal finance games as a way to create tuition money. And it contributes to frequent rule changes as Uncle tries to find ways to prevent low life from abusing the system (For example, defaults on student loans will cost nearly $3.6 billion next year!).

Uncle needs close watching. To watch him intelligently, you should develop a working acquaintance with "authorizations," "appropriations," "budget reconciliations," "Federal Regulations," and "rescissions." Better still, read the new edition of this book which comes out every fall. We'll do the Uncle-watching for you.

TREND C: COLLEGES WANT YOU

There is a sunny side to the declining student population. Colleges now want you, more than ever before. Your parents may still think in terms of great college selectivity, however, for all but about 100 schools, selectivity is out the window. The operating word is "survival." Today, approximately 80% of students are accepted by the institutions to which they apply. The seller's market has become a buyer's market. It widens your opportunity to shop wisely and well. And the more marketable you are—good grades, leadership, musical talent, athletic ability—the more college-sponsored financial aid opportunities you will find.

One caution: Under pressure to recruit students, expect college materials to become slicker in execution. There will be a greater willingness, on the part of colleges, to tell you about their own strengths and their competitors' weaknesses. In their efforts to attract the best and the brightest, colleges have used advertising, direct mail, and phone solicitation. Many have even turned to professional filmmakers (at $30,000 - $50,000 a shot) for a more direct, emotional sales pitch. Some schools spend as much as $800 per freshman actually enrolled.

Don't be too critical of schools for these practices. Their survival may be at stake. But do raise your consumer guards and evaluate collegiate mass-marketing techniques with the same objectivity and skepticism you normally reserve for television advertisements and mass-marketing techniques originating from other sources.

TREND D: TUITION AID IN RETURN FOR SERVICES

The nation needs more teachers. How can it stimulate interest in this field yet continue to pay teachers minuscule wages? Easy. Provide loans to prospective teachers. If the recipients actually go into teaching, the loans are "forgiven." But, if the recipients decide, after graduation, that working in a bike shop would be more rewarding than teaching math, the loan money must be repaid, with interest. Federal and state versions of this program have become common. Also expect to see the concept extended to any and all fields that can be stimulated by educational incentives that are cheaper than paying a competitive salary.

Recent surveys show our nation also needs to stimulate its social conscience; materialism is on the rise. Accordingly, several bills have been introduced to encourage "volunteerism" in exchange for tuition assistance. These will be discussed in Chapter 10.

TREND E: GROWING CASH FLOW PROBLEMS, GROWING CASH FLOW HELP

When tuitions rise faster than available student aid, parents and students must make up the difference. But this is not a "vive la difference" to be cheered. It is a nasty cash flow problem that can and will grow worse with each passing year. A cash flow problem, in case you don't understand, comes about when you have the money to pay the bills, but the money is not "liquid." It is tied up in assets like your house, and you certainly don't want to sell your house.

But take heart. Problems create solutions. Financial innovators are coming up with plans that will help with the cash flow without requiring you to place a "For Sale" sign in front of the family castle. For instance, several states have raised money on the tax-exempt bond market for no other purpose than to make low-interest college loans. Banks and brokerage houses have credit lines that permit flexible borrowing against your home equity. A planner in Atlanta has designed an ingenious savings/borrowing plan that applies leverage principles to your funds. Colleges themselves are becoming lenders, providing long-term loans at adjustable interest rates.

A lot is going on. And, we'll cover it at the precise point in this book when you throw up your hands and say, "We can't do it. No Way." We figure this will come around Chapter 7.

TREND F: FINANCIAL PLANNERS TO THE RESCUE

Personal finance experts appear under many guises—stockbrokers, financial planners, bankers, accountants, and insurance people. Many of these people are bright, resourceful professionals who can be of genuine help in the college financing process. Unfortunately, some of them are good at planning only one thing—their own lucrative retirement. Before you enlist in any of their services, ask some questions. *Are they fee only planners or do they work on commission?* Fee only planners charge by the hour. While this may cost you more money in the short-run, fee only planners point out that their counterparts don't always have real incentives to provide you with totally unbiased service (i.e., some planners on commission will give you nothing but a glossy sales pitch for whatever products bring the largest commission). *What are their fields of expertise?* Your planner should be familiar with investment strategies of all types— traditional advice on retirement planning and estate planning is not necessarily compatible with sound college planning. Your advisor should be able to explain these possible conflicts and help you maximize all of your resources (while minimizing your tax consequences). *What is their prior work experience?* Did they get their start in insurance? A brokerage house? A college financial aid office? Charm school? *What are their professional credentials?* Do they still have ties to an insurance company or brokerage house? Are they with a reputable company such as IDS (a division of American Express)? Have they been certified by a reputable group such as The Institute of Certified Financial Planners or The College for Financial Planning? *Is the planner providing you with a service you can't get from your accountant or your lawyer?* There is no sense in paying for the same service twice. **Finally, ask for references: Reputable planners don't want to be confused with the scam artists and will be only too happy to oblige.**

TREND G: FASCINATION WITH EXCELLENCE

Major studies have aroused public opinion about the decline of excellence in elementary and secondary schools. Every solution suggested requires tons of money. Lengthen the school day. Lengthen the school year. Pay some teachers more than others. Pay all teachers more. Plug a computer into every socket. Not all solutions will be adopted. But some will, and money will flow. In a finite economy, that money must come from somewhere. Most likely, it will come from money that otherwise might have gone to financing your higher education.

But again, there is a sunny side. The enshrining of excellence legitimates the use of academic scholarships, on the part of colleges, to attract high-performance students. Expect continued growth in such awards.

TREND H: A COLLEGE EDUCATION STILL PAYS

A college education will prepare you for a fulfilling life—through broader culture awareness, deeper knowledge, greater self-confidence, sounder health, richer pleasures, keener citizenship and vastly expanded resources for personal happiness.

If philosophical reasons aren't enough, and we've already mentioned the reported rise in materialism among college bound students, you'll be pleased to learn that college still helps you earn more money. Here are some recent figures from the US Bureau of the Census (with great restraint, the author reserves comment on the income differential between men and women until Chapter 22):

Highest Education Completed	*Average Annual Income—Men*	*Average Annual Income—Women*
High School	$18,936	$ 9,420
College	$33,324	$16,656
Master's	$39,924	$25,176
Professional	$58,080	$29,928

Chapter 2
Common Myths & Misconceptions & Mistakes

Practically everyone we know equates the search for monetary help for college with a search for scholarships. Get rid of that belief quickly! And repeat after us three times: To obtain financial aid, sophisticated families:

- Present the family's situation for need analysis in the most favorable terms legally allowed.
- Apply to all the major assistance programs for which they are eligible.
- Apply early, accurately and honestly.
- Select a college that is more likely than others to present them with a good financial aid package.
- When appropriate, discuss with the financial aid officer the possibility of improving the aid that was offered.
- Become knowledgeable of favorable options—commercial or otherwise—for financing educational expenses not covered by aid awards.

These steps can be worth thousands of dollars. Any other approach will make you the unknowing looking for the unfindable. You will gain nothing, while paying out plenty—in wasted time and money. Now read this short chapter on the myths, misconceptions, fables and folklore that envelop the financial aid field. And remember: You don't profit from these beliefs; only the people who keep them alive do.

WON'T A SCHOLARSHIP REPLACE MY MONEY?

Most people believe that scholarships will put money in their pocket. Example: You have been assessed a $5,000 per year contribution to College X, a school that costs more than that to attend. One lucky day, you win a $1,000 scholarship. You now say your contribution will be $4,000. Right? Wrong. Your contribution will still be $5,000. The college takes the $1,000 and incorporates it into your financial aid package where it may replace a loan or a work opportunity or a grant that the college had planned on using to help you. The colleges have another option—not used as often—for handling your award. They can decide that the scholarship increases your available resources. Instead of a $5,000 contribution, you are now capable of making a $6,000 contribution. **The scholarship, in other words, will help pay your college bill but it will not reduce your share of the bill.**

If that is so, you may ask, then why do clubs and organizations work so hard to raise scholarship money to help a particular student? The answer: They are not familiar with college financial aid packaging techniques. If they were, all that money raised by candy bar sales and church suppers would go to a different purpose.

Another question. Why do colleges urge students to find scholarships? Every college catalogue suggests that students check with their guidance office or visit their public library. The answer: The scholarship you bring to the college will, in effect, free some of the college's money that had been earmarked to help you. It can now use that money to help another student. What results, in fact, is that the scholarship won by Student A will actually benefit Student B. This may not have been the donor's intention, but it is a generous act and should not go unnoticed. Remember: It's only the money that goes to the other student. You, the winner, retain the honor.

LOOKING FOR SPECIAL SCHOLARSHIPS

Every day we get letters from people who give us their age, sex, race, career intentions, physical condition and personal finance data and then ask "is there a special scholarship for me?" These letters sadden us, because we know the writers haven't followed the normal route for getting financial aid.

Here is what we reply, "Please don't waste your time looking for a special award for a (black, white, red) 35-year-old, seeking to return to the labor force as a sorcerer's apprentice. Most financial aid is based on financial need and student status. If college costs more than your assessed contribution, you are eligible for financial aid. Your age, sex, race and career ambitions have nothing to do with it."

Even if you do find a "special scholarship" source, remember, there's a world of difference between being eligible and winning. For example, the 4-H program offers approximately 280 awards, but with nearly 500,000 high school seniors as members, your odds of winning are only 1785:1. To increase your chances, you may have purchase a one-week old piglet, feed it 20 times a day until it weighs 1700 pounds. Then you have to rent a forklift and a truck, take it to the state fair, and hope it wins a blue ribbon in the heavy hog competition. This might improve your odds of winning to 20 or 30 to 1. But what about the costs of raising a 1700 pound porker?

Our advice: Go the traditional financial aid route (Parts II and III) first. Then, if you have a lot of time and nothing else to do, and you need practice writing letters and you feel you must help the U.S. Postal Service stay in the black, start looking for a "special scholarship." You may even find one.

UNCLAIMED SCHOLARSHIPS

Q. I have read that millions of dollars in scholarship funds go unclaimed every year. Is this true?

A. If you believe this, you probably also believe you'll win a $100 million lottery jackpot (at odds of 9.6 million to 1). According to actuarial expert Dr. Jean Lemaire (the Wharton School, the University of Pennsylvania), you'd have a better chance of living past the age of 115! Seriously, a few dollars in college aid does go unclaimed, but according to most financial aid professionals, the millions you hear about are unused employee tuition benefits. See below.

SCHOLARSHIPS FROM CORPORATIONS & FOUNDATIONS

Q. I have heard that big corporations offer a lot of scholarships.

A. Many do—to the children of their employees. If your mom works for Westinghouse, you might get help. If your dad works in the neighborhood barbershop—forget it! Some corporations have awards for other than their employees' children. These are usually administered by colleges which in turn select the recipients. You can't apply for them directly.

Q. What about foundations?

A. Mainly, they help students at the doctoral or post-doctoral level. There is also some money for the college-bound and undergraduates. But that money usually has very narrow local restrictions, e.g., for students in Teenytiny County. Normally, such localized foundation grants are well publicized on the school bulletin board and in the local paper. But if they aren't and you don't want to miss any of these opportunities, then spend some time in the public library with a reference book called *Foundation Grants to Individuals*.

COMPUTERIZED SCHOLARSHIP SEARCHES

If you need information on federal or state student aid, don't pay a computer service. You can learn all you need to know from this book or the free pamphlets that Uncle Sam and your state government hand out.

If you need information on student aid offered by the colleges to which you are applying, don't pay a computer service. The college catalogue will tell you what you need to know.

If you need information on scholarships offered by your employer or church, don't pay a computer service. Ask your boss or minister.

If you need information on local scholarships, don't pay a computer service. Check the high school bulletin board.

Most experts in financial aid agree; computerized scholarship services are not likely to be of much help in your search for private aid sources.

TRUSTS, GIFTS AND OTHER DEVICES CAN BE HAZARDOUS TO YOUR COLLEGE BILLS

Many people can't accept the fact they are in a higher tax bracket than their children. They will shift assets from themselves to their offspring, thinking the income from these assets will then be taxed at a much lower rate.

Such transfers used to take the simple form of a deposit into junior's savings account. Then, people became more sophisticated and used devices such as Clifford Trusts and Spousal Remainder Trusts—both of which had to be constructed with the help of lawyers and accountants whose fees could run upwards of $500.

Then, when the new tax laws passed, all this maneuvering went for naught. Investment income in excess of $1100 for children under 14 is now taxed at the parents rate, as is all income from Clifford Trusts and Spousal Remainder Trusts. What was left for families to do? Pay financial planners even more money to tell them how to get out of their current fiscal mess.

In short, some schemes devised by financial planners should carry a big red warning label that says, "This Device May Be Hazardous To Your College Bills." You'll understand why after you have read Chapters 7 and 8.

READING THE WRONG REFERENCES

Everybody knows that Lasser's Income Tax Guide takes a somewhat different slant to its subject than the publications from IRS. Lasser's objective is to show you ways to save on taxes while the IRS seeks to extract the last drop of blood. You may value the IRS guide for its mechanical instructions, but not for its substantive advice on holding on to more of your money.

It's the same with paying-for-college guides. Before you purchase one or read one, make sure you know the guide's origin. Is it written from the viewpoint of those who pay the money (parents or students)? Is it written by those who get the money (colleges and collegiate organizations)? Or is it written by those who give the money (Uncle Sam and the states)? The guides may treat the same subject, but their treatment could be many dollars (your dollars) apart.

READING OLD REFERENCES

In student financial aid, any reference older than one year is out of date. If you use an older reference, you will be badly misled with regard to loan sources, interest rates, aid eligibilities, grants size, saving techniques, government regulations, and college costs.

Chapter 3
Using this Guide

ORGANIZATION OF GUIDE

The sequence of topics in the rest of this guide parallels the steps you should take in your quest for college financing. First, you must define your monetary need and second, you must learn how to finance that need.

We ask that you do not skip to the resources listed at end of the book and begin firing off appeals for help. Chances are good that it will be a waste of your time and the time of the kind organizations offering assistance.

Instead, start at the beginning.

In Part II of this book you will learn the special vocabulary of financial aid. You will meet the players in the financial aid game, and you will develop an understanding of their roles and interests and come to appreciate that these interests may not always be the same as yours. Also, in Part II, you will learn how to calculate your family contribution—the amount of money your family is judged capable of contributing to college costs. We will guide you through the entire aid application process and show you how to take charge of each step along the way.

Why is taking charge important?

1. It increases your eligibility for aid.
2. It enhances your chances of receiving all the aid to which you are entitled.
3. It improves the composition of your award, meaning more scholarships and fewer loans.
4. It gives you a major advantage over those who enter the process passively, without understanding what is being done to them.
5. It gives you a gargantuan advantage over those who drift through the process in complete confusion.
6. It gives you an infinite advantage over those who don't enter the process at all.

In Part III, you move from the fundamentals to more advanced approaches. You become a financial aid whiz who masters all the moves in the financial aid game—college selection, personal finance techniques, and tax strategies. You will learn the best moves for each of two different situations: (1) when college entrance is approaching fast and (2) when college is still years away.

In Part IV, you will meet the major money sources—the colleges, Uncle Sam, and the states. They are the dispensers of billions of dollars. By getting to know their programs well, you will not overlook a single penny that is due you.

Part V introduces you to two major alternatives for financing college costs—your boss, and the US military. The suggestions offered may not be to your liking, but you should know about them and consider or reject them at this point in the decision process.

Part VI groups special opportunities. You've already had the meat and potatoes course. Now you are looking for the cake or maybe just the frosting. You'll find sections here for the bright and for the career-oriented, for the athlete and for the graduate student, for minorities and for women, and for the handicapped. One or more of these special opportunities are bound to fit your situation and round out your meal. The tips at the end of Part VI bring together many of the ideas and suggestions developed earlier at greater length. Use these tips as a review.

There is no Part VII. But if there was, it would be an award ceremony where we present you with the title of "Financial Aid Guru."

Part II
The Fundamentals of Financial Aid

Chapter 4
Definitions & Players

Grants and Scholarships are aid awards that do not have to be repaid. They are gifts. Some scholarships, though not all, will require you to perform a service. The recipient of a band scholarship, for instance, will have to dress up in a funny costume complete with spats, march around a football field, and blow into a piccolo or tuba whenever the college so directs.

Loans are sums of money that must be repaid. To qualify as financial aid, loans must carry an interest charge that is lower than prevailing commercial rates. They must also offer favorable repayment provisions. An example of favorable repayment provisions: the Stafford Student Loan. Borrowers do not start paying interest on the loan nor do they have to retire any of the principal until six months after completing their studies.

Work counts as financial aid when employment is arranged for you through the financial aid office. Earnings from work you found yourself are not included as part of financial aid. Such earnings are added to the sum you are judged capable of contributing to college costs.

Enrollment Status impacts on aid eligibility. To qualify for some federal student aid (such as Pell Grants and Stafford Student Loans) as well as state aid and money from the college, you must be at least a half-time student. Half-time is generously defined. It consists of six semester or quarter hours per academic term for schools on the semester, quarter, or trimester system; 12 semester hours or 18 quarter hours per school year for schools that use a credit hour system; or 12 clock hours a week for schools that use clock hours to measure course programs.

Under this system, a $1,000 award for a full-time student becomes a $750 award for a three-quarter-time student (one majoring in the waltz?) and $500 for a half-time student. Even programs authorized to award financial aid to less-than-half-time students, only do so if there are extra funds (i.e., if the money will be taken from someone else who needs it). This scenario is not likely. **A tip:** If you are a part-time student and wish to qualify for aid, take one more course each semester.

Satisfactory Academic Progress by the end of your sophomore year is necessary to maintain aid eligibility. The definition of this euphoric stage has recently been articulated by Congress to mean a cumulative "C" average or academic standing consistent with the individual institution's requirements for graduation. A tip: If you are uneasy about making the transition from high school to the faster, academic pace of colleges, don't overload yourself. Start light until you become acclimatized. That way you protect not only your grades but also your aid award.

Accreditation is a process that ensures the school's programs maintain at least a minimum level of quality. Make sure the school you plan to attend has been accredited by a nationally recognized accreditation association. Not only do you not want to waste your tuition dollars getting a worthless education, but students who attend a non-accredited school will not qualify for federal or state student aid.

THE 1ST PLAYER—THE STUDENT

Students may see themselves as "A" students or "C" students, as freshmen or juniors, as jocks or dweebs, as hot or not.

Financial aid programs have their own classification system that defines students by dependency status. They are either independent students or dependent students.

A dependent student is one who is at least partially dependent on his or her parents for support.

The income and assets of both student and parent are used to develop the amount a family must contribute to college costs.

An independent student is not dependent on parental support. Only the student's income and assets (and that of any relevant spouse) are evaluated to determine the contribution to college costs. An independent student may also be classified as a dislocated worker or displaced homemaker as defined below ("The 2nd Player—The Parent").

To be considered independent, under federal regulations, a student must meet one of the following conditions:

1. Be 24 years of age by December 31 of the award year (e.g., December 31, 1992 for the 1992/93 award year).
2. Be an orphan, ward of the court, or a veteran of the Armed Services.
3. Have legal dependents other than a spouse.
4. Be married, a professional student, or a graduate students, and not be claimed as a tax exemption by his or her parents for the first calendar year of the award year (e.g., 1992 for the 1992/93 award year).
5. Be a single undergraduate, under the age of 24, with no dependents and not claimed as a dependent for tax purposes by his or her parents for either of the two calendar years preceding the award year (e.g., 1990 and 1991 for the 1992/93 award year). Furthermore, a person in this category must demonstrate self-sufficiency by showing an income of at least $4000 in each of those two years.
6. Be judged independent by the financial aid officer based on documented unusual circumstances.

Establishing independence gives you an advantage: By not having to include parental income and assets on your financial aid application forms, your college contribution will most likely be lower and that will result in more student aid.

To preserve scarce aid funds, most states and almost all colleges have gone beyond the federal test to impose additional restrictions on your declaration of independence. These include written proof that the student's parents (or even grandparents) cannot provide any support whatsoever.

Now an important point: Once you have established independence, don't give it up. It will cost you money when you think it may be saving you money. Here is an example: George Webber, a young writer and truly independent student, decides to go back to college. He moves into his parents' home to save on room and board. His parents are thrilled by the extra tax exemption. What happened? He became dependent again. His parents, who thought they had picked up just another mouth to feed, found themselves again involved in footing tuition bills, only now the money came from their pension checks. Dad had to pawn his fishing pole. Mom had to sell her golf clubs. Both were furious. The sad lesson: Heed Thomas Wolfe, "You Can't Go Home Again."

Another important point: If you start college receiving financial aid as a dependent student, as long as you're a single undergraduate under the age of 24, you can't get your status changed to independent, regardless of how much you earn or whether your parents claim you on their taxes (except, of course, under special conditions).

THE 2ND PLAYER—THE PARENTS

Parents may be sweet, loving, caring, supportive role models. The financial aid process could care less. Its main interest: Are they married, separated, divorced? Is there a stepparent around who can foot the bill?

Here is the impact of marital status on financial aid:

Both Parents Are Alive and Married to Each Other. The income and assets of both parents are fair pickings for the financial aid computer.

Parents Are Divorced Or Separated. Financial aid forms are interested in the income and assets of the parent with whom the student lived for the majority of the calendar year preceding the academic year for which the aid is requested. The form is not interested in the other parent.

A Parent Remarries. If the parent with whom the student lived the greater part of the calendar year remarries, the stepparent automatically assumes partial responsibility for the student. His or her income and assets are evaluated for a contribution to college costs as though he or she were a natural parent.

The financial aid process also cares about the parent's (or independent student's) employment status. It gives special consideration to what it calls "displaced homemakers" and "dislocated workers." Chapter 6 explains in more detail how these groups fare under the Congressional Methodology, but here is an explanation of the categories.

A Parent (or Independent Student) is a Displaced Homemaker. According to Uncle Sam's vague definition, a displaced homemaker is an individual who meets all of the following requirements:
1. Has been out of the labor force for a "substantial number of years" (e.g., five years) but who during those years has worked in the home providing unpaid services for family members, AND
2. Has lost his or her source of income (whether it was public assistance or the income of another family member) or is receiving public assistance because of dependent children still in the home, AND
3. Is unemployed or underemployed and is having trouble getting or upgrading a job.

A Parent (or Independent Student) is a Dislocated Worker. This category is defined by individual state agencies in accordance with Title III of the Job Training Partnership Act. To see if a parent qualifies, check with your state's employment service. In general, however, "dislocated worker" refers to an individual who has been:
1. Fired OR
2. Laid off as part of a permanent factory closing OR
3. Self-employed (including farmers) but is now unemployed because of a natural disaster or poor economic conditions within the community.

The rules we have described apply to federal aid and, generally, to state aid. The colleges, when they decide how to dispense their own money, are not bound by these rules. They will frequently probe deeply into the resources of the divorced and absent parent who got off scot-free under federal regulations.

THE 3RD PLAYER—THE COLLEGES

We'll say a lot more about colleges in Chapter 9. At this time, you should know that colleges can be classified as either private or public.

Private colleges can be more innovative in developing attractive college financing schemes and tuition assistance programs. They are not as circumscribed by red tape as are tax-supported schools.

Private colleges also have more latitude in how to spend their money. Again, it's their money, not the taxpayer's.

Public colleges, however, being tax-supported, are usually less expensive. As a general rule, students are seldom asked to pay more then 30% of actual tuition costs. The state pays the balance.

Also, public colleges have two sets of fee structures: a lower one for state residents and a higher one for out-of-state students. At one time, it was easy to establish state residency to qualify for the lower rate. Today, it's getting difficult. Most states have erected elaborate defense structures seemingly manned with beady-eyed, cold-hearted officials whose efficiency appears to be judged in direct proportion to the number of residency denials issued.

One more thing. Private and public colleges have no great love for one another. The lack of affection is rooted in money. The privates resent the subsidies that permit the public schools to offer lower tuitions. They would dearly love to end this "unfair competition" by qualifying for subsidies of their own. Moreover, they see their own turf invaded when public schools, not fully sated by subsidies, seek funds from philanthropies or establish foundations that let them get around the rather inflexible expenditure guidelines imposed by the states. The public schools, for their part, have kept quiet. They know it is smarter to keep your mouth shut when you're ahead. Some of this hostility ends when the two must present a united front (strength in numbers) to keep Congress from going along with the Administration's repeated efforts to slash the education budget.

THE 4TH PLAYER—THE NEED ANALYSIS SERVICES

Before the colleges can consider you for aid, they must know how much you can pay. The family that can pay $10,000 won't be eligible for as much aid as the family that can spare only $1,000.

Determining how much you can pay, without becoming a burden to your neighbors, is called **Need Analysis**. The job is performed by agencies known as Need Analysis Services (or, in bureaucratese, Multiple Data Entry—MDE—processors). Their tool is a longish form called a financial aid application (or Multiple Data Entry—MDE—application).

The chief need analysis services are the College Board's College Scholarship Service (Princeton, NJ) which serves schools on the East and West Coasts and the American College Testing Program (Iowa City, IA) which is big in the Midwest and the South. The other two approved services are United Student Aid Funds (Indianapolis, IN) and the PA Higher Education Assistance Agency (Harrisburg, PA).

The services use an identical evaluation technique in going over your family finances. Because the formula is mandated by Congress, it is known as the Congressional Methodology. You would gain nothing by submitting your data to one service rather than the other. In fact, the core of each form (the part that calculates eligibility for federal student aid programs) must even be identical in appearance. So why are there five different processors? States and colleges like to have additional knowledge about your family's finances to determine eligibility for their own programs. Each processor, therefore, collects "supplemental material" to meet the needs of these, their real clients.

The Congressional Methodology, incidentally, is just one method of need analysis, albeit the most important. Others you will encounter both in this book and in real life include the Pell Grant Methodology and the Simplified Needs Test.

THE FIFTH PLAYER—THE FINANCIAL AID OFFICER

If money is water and you are a basin, the financial aid officer is the faucet (Yes, I know. There will be letters from financial aid officers who object to this metaphor. They would rather be likened to the valiant Hector rallying the warriors of ancient Troy. Well, maybe "faucet" is a bad word. Would "spigot" or "nozzle" be better?).

For the college-bound and those in college, the financial aid officer can be the most important person on campus.

The FAO can take the family contribution cranked out by the need analysis services and—ouch—increase it or—hurray—reduce it.

The FAO can draw on money under the college's control or certify the student's eligibility for money not under the school's direct control.

The FAO can decide on the contents of the student's assistance package. Is it to be scholarships and grants that do not have to be repaid? Or will it all be in loans?

In short, the FAO is the final arbiter of how much the family must contribute to college costs and how much outside help, and of what kind, the family will receive.

Get to know this player. He or she can make the difference between winning and losing.

Chapter 5
This You Must Understand

Ubi Est Mea (Old Latin Proverb, Translation: Where is Mine?)

THE CONCEPT OF NEED

In a recent survey, The Council for Advancement and Support of Education (CASE) discovered that 49% of high school students believed they could not receive financial aid for an expensive private school if their parents could afford to send them to a state school. Thirty-three percent believed that almost all financial aid was set aside for minority students.

Of course, neither of these assumptions is true.

All financial aid is based on the concept of "need." You cannot understand financial aid without understanding "need."

Need should never be confused with "needy."

Need is a number—nothing more, nothing less.

This is how to determine the need number:

Visualize two bars, Bar A and Bar B. Bar A will represent your family's contribution to college costs, as determined by need analysis (see previous chapter). Bar B is the cost of attendance at the college of your choice.

Bar A—your contribution—is a constant (unless there is a drastic change in your family's situation). It doesn't matter where you plan to buy your education. The amount you must contribute from your own purse will be the same. Bar B—the cost of attendance—is a variable. It will vary from college to college. It can even vary within one school, depending on your student status, the courses you take, how far away you live, etc.

If Bar A is smaller than Bar B, you have financial need.

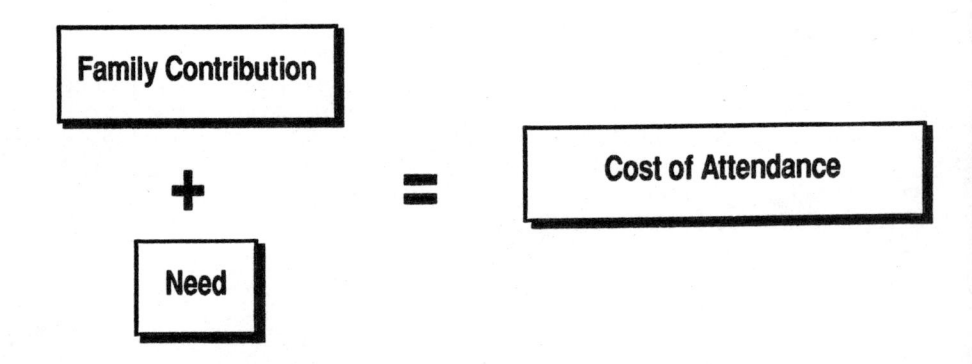

Family Contribution + Need = Cost of Attendance

Let's illustrate this concept of need for a family judged capable of contributing $5,000 per year to college costs and considers three colleges, College X which costs $15,000; College Y which costs $8,000; and College Z which costs $4,000:

At College X, that family's need is $10,000; at College Y it is $3,000; and at College Z the family has no need at all.

College X

| $5,000 | $10,000 |

| $15,000 |

College Y

| $5,000 | $3,000 |

| $8,000 |

College Z

| $5,000 |

| $4,000 |

REMAINING NEED

To understand financial aid fully, you must understand one more concept: Remaining Need. Remaining Need will determine whether you qualify for a low-interest, Stafford Student Loan (formerly called a Guaranteed Student Loan—See Chapter 10).

Remaining need equals the cost of attendance at the college of your choice minus your family contribution and any aid you receive. Let's use a bar diagram to illustrate this concept.

You plan to attend College X which costs $15,000 per year. Your family contribution has been judged to be $5,000. The college will provide you with $3,000 in grants, $2,000 in Perkins Loans, $1,000 in work-study, and you have found a $1,000 scholarship. Thus, you have $7,000 in assistance. Your Remaining Need is $3,000. Calculation: $15,000-($5,000 + $3,000 +$2,000+ $1,000 + $1,000) = $3,000.

| $15,000 | = | $5,000 | $7,000 | $3,000 |

Cost of Attendance   **Family Contribution**   **Aid**   **Remaining Need**

Important: Don't think the two elements that enter into the need calculation—the family contribution and the college cost of attendance—are carved in stone.

They are elastic. They can be stretched and they can be squeezed. This is not the time to show you how to turn rock into play-doh. But it is time to let you know it can be done. In Chapter 7 you will find a plethora of ideas for stretching and squeezing.

Chapter 6
Taking Charge of the Link-Up Process

WHY TAKE CHARGE?

The college admission and financial aid cycles operate on different schedules. You select colleges in the fall, apply during the winter, and hope to get an acceptance decision in early spring.

The financial aid cycle, however, cannot be formally initiated until after the first of the year in which you plan to attend college (so the computers can be fed exact information on how much your family earned the previous year). You submit your financial aid application as soon as after January 1 as possible. Then you are kept in the dark for several months before you learn (1) how much you will have to contribute, (2) whether you have need and (3) whether you qualify for need-based aid.

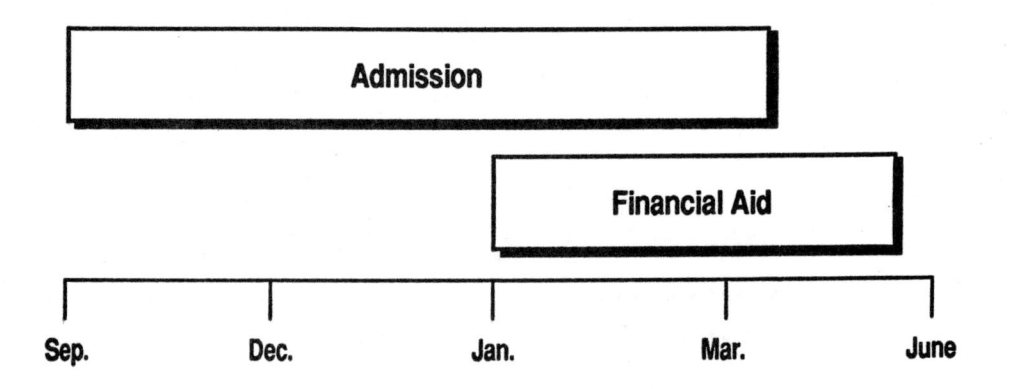

```
|-------------------Admission-------------------|
                          |----Financial Aid----|
Sep.      Dec.      Jan.            Mar.      June
```

As you can see, you shop for colleges before you know your out-of-pocket costs, the size of your contribution, and the amount of help for which you are eligible.

If you want to assume your family contribution, once you learn what it is, will not cause you a cash-flow problem, and that your need will be met at whatever college you elect to attend, then you can trust the system and submit all your applications in the dark.

You would then be like the good soldier who does what he is told, when he is told; who carries out all orders, even though he does not understand them.

But if you assume, realistically, that (1) your family contribution will impose a cash-flow burden, (2) your need will not be met in all cases or (3) if it is met, it may be met in a manner that may be financially burdensome to you, you cannot be a good soldier. You have to take charge of the process. In doing so, you protect your own interests. You guard against shocks and surprises. You allot adequate planning time. You improve your chances of having all your need met and met in an attractive manner. You may even succeed in lowering your family contribution and qualifying for more aid.

If you don't take charge, you will be as helpless as a jellyfish, bobbing in the waves, drifting where the tides take you. Eventually you will be soaked in brine and gobbled up by a killer whale.

What does all this mean? Let's translate these general statements into specifics to illustrate each point:

Your Objective	The Good Soldier	The Take-Charge Applicant
To guard against shock.	Won't learn of family contribution until late spring. Will be surprised by amount. Has little time to raise the money and may be forced to change college plans.	Knows from the start how much college will cost family. Has almost one year to figure out how to raise money.
Make sure size of aid package corresponds to need.	When selecting colleges, does not consider their ability to meet family's need fully.	Makes schools' ability to meet need part of college selection and application strategy.
Get an attractive aid package; one that's rich in grants and low on loans.	When selecting colleges, does not consider their ability to present an attractive aid package.	Makes schools' ability to present an attractive aid package part of college selection and application strategy.

WHAT IS MEANT BY TAKING CHARGE?

Taking charge is not complex. You won't have to enroll in a leadership or muscle-building course or graduate from Infantry Officer Candidate School. All you have to do is read this chapter and the next and act on the advice they give you.

The take-charge process has three elements:

1. **Learn the Money Numbers Ahead of Time.** Even before you fill out any financial aid applications, you should have a good idea of (1) the size of your family contribution, (2) the attendance costs at the colleges of your choice, and (3) the amount of need you will have at each of these schools.
2. **Execute the Mechanics of the Application Process With Speed and Precision.** That's how you insure you'll be first in line for aid, before the "Sold Out" and "No Vacancy" signs go up.
3. **Know About Influence Points.** College selection, preparing yourself for need analysis, the speed and accuracy with which you apply, the evaluation of aid offers, financial aid officers—these are all influence points. How you handle yourself as you approach these points will impact on your family contribution, aid eligibility, and size and composition of your aid award.

ANSWERS TO THREE QUESTIONS

Let's begin with the first element of the take-charge process: Knowing the Money Numbers Ahead of Time. You do that by securing answers to three questions:

1. How much will our family be expected to contribute to college costs? This, you remember, is a constant.
2. What are the annual costs of attendance at the college(s) of my choice? This is the variable.
3. What's our need going to be at each college of my choice?

Once you have the answer to Question #3—even if it's just an approximation—you can begin some sensible financial planning.

QUESTION #1: HOW MUCH WILL WE HAVE TO PAY?

Family Contribution is made up of two elements: the Parents' Contribution and the Student's Contribution (if you are an independent student, the Family Contribution will correspond to the Student's Contribution). Family contribution is calculated by the need analysis services (see chapter 4).

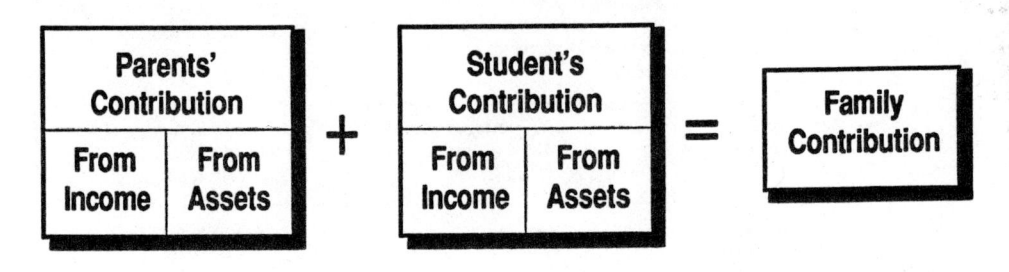

```
┌─────────────────────┐         ┌─────────────────────┐         ┌─────────────────────┐
│      Parents'       │         │      Student's      │         │                     │
│    Contribution     │    +    │    Contribution     │    =    │       Family        │
├─────────┬───────────┤         ├─────────┬───────────┤         │    Contribution     │
│  From   │   From    │         │  From   │   From    │         │                     │
│ Income  │  Assets   │         │ Income  │  Assets   │         │                     │
└─────────┴───────────┘         └─────────┴───────────┘         └─────────────────────┘
```

To complicate matters some, three different need analysis systems will be in operation for the 92/93 school year.

All systems operate on the same principle. They let you shelter some of your money for taxes, living expenses and retirement. Then they want what is left.

You should know that the family maintenance allowance—the money left to you for shelter, food, clothing, car operations, insurance and basic medical care—is based on the Department of Labor's "low budget standard." If you have gotten along on a low budget standard, the need analysis formula will fit you like a glove. But if you have become locked into a higher standard of living, with larger mortgage payments, fatter utility bills, two cars, summer vacations, an occasional trip to the theater, and so on, the small allowance won't do you. It won't cover expenses. And your assessed family contribution will appear impossibly large!

Need Analysis System	Programs Served
Congressional Methodology	1. The colleges' own resources 2. Many state programs 3. Private donor programs 4. Uncle Sam's campus-based programs (Perkins, SEOG, CW-s) 5. Stafford Student Loans
Simplified Need Test	Same as above
Pell Grant Methodology	Pell Grants

- **The Congressional Methodology** is the system that will, more than any other, impact on your eligibility for student aid. It should concern you the most. Incidentally, 95% of all financial aid officers, in a response to a survey, indicated they did not think parents and students understood need analysis. Can you imagine that? Plunking down $50,000 or $100,000 for an education and not knowing how your share of that cost is assessed! You, as one of our readers, will be in the 5% who know.
- **The Simplified Need Test** may be used by families whose total adjusted gross incomes (including the student, spouse and parents incomes) are under $15,000 and who file a 1040EZ, a 1040A, or who do not file a tax return at all. The simplified formula is essentially

the same as the Congressional Methodology with the following exceptions; assets are not considered and no allowance is made for medical/dental expenses or elementary/secondary tuition payments.

The Pell Grant Methodology relates only to Pell Grant eligibility. Generally, a family of four with income of $35,000 or more and assets of $42,000 is at the eligibility cut-off line. Families with lesser income should qualify for a slice of the Pell Grant pie.

Now it's time to calculate the family contribution under the Congressional Methodology. Dependent Students go to Appendix 1. Independent Students go to Appendix 2 or 3. Dislocated workers, displaced homemakers and those eligible for simplified needs analysis should calculate their contribution first using the "full-data" Congressional Methodology as it appears in the appendices, and then again, filling in only the items necessary for their situation (as marked in the appropriate appendix). Decide which is more advantageous. In any case, the end product of your calculations won't match to the penny what the need analysis computer will determine. But the result will be in the ball park. Note: You should also run a need analysis check under the Pell Grant Methodology. For that you must use *College Grants From Uncle Sam* (see inside back cover).

Here are some things to know before you start filling in the figures:

Dependent Students
- All income and tax data comes from the previous calendar year. If you start college in September 1992, the previous calendar year is 1991.
- All asset data is as of the date you submit the need analysis form.
- If your parents are divorced or separated, use the income and asset figures of the parent with whom you lived for the greater part of the previous calendar year.
- If your parent has remarried and if your stepparent declares you as a dependent, you must include his or her income and asset information.

Independent Student
- All income and tax data comes from the previous calendar year. If you start college in September 1992, the previous calendar year is 1991.
- All asset data is as of the date you submit the need analysis form.

Dislocated Workers and Displaced Homemakers
If you, one of your parents, or your spouse is a dislocated worker or displaced homemaker (See Chapter 4), the following modifications can be made when calculating your expected family contribution (FC).

1. Dislocated workers who file the "full data" financial aid application, may use expected income (1992 for the 1992/93 award year) rather than previous year income (1991) to calculate FC. For dislocated workers who qualify for the simplified need test, please note: You must record previous year income, not expected income; there are no dislocated worker variations in the simplified formula.
2. Both dislocated workers and displaced homemakers may exclude home assets in the calculation of FC.

All of this is horribly confusing and is only important because in some cases, the family contribution for these two groups will actually be lower by not taking advantage of the above mentioned modifications. Here's why: Contribution from assets can be a negative and thereby offset some of the contribution from income. In these instances, it would be advantageous NOT to use the simplified form. Here's our recommendation, even if you qualify for the simplified formula, file the full data application. You will then receive two family contribution figures; a primary figure based on the simplified test and a secondary based on the full data formula.

An Important Point

Question. Why should I calculate the family contribution myself? The high school guidance office has a computer program that will make the calculation. I also understand that many college recruiters lug a portable computer around that will make the calculation.

Answer. Getting a number and accepting it casts you in the passive role colleges want you to assume in the financial aid application process. But getting that same number by calculating it yourself is part of the take-charge drill.

By making the calculation you will develop an appreciation of the formula, its components, and the weights assigned to each component. When you combine this knowledge with the "advanced information" provided in the next chapter, you will get ideas for rearranging family financial data so as to obtain the most favorable analysis possible. And that can be worth a lot of money. Also, an intimate knowledge of the formula's components will serve you well, later in the cycle, if you should have to discuss your aid award, and its calculation, with a financial aid officer.

QUESTION #2: HOW MUCH WILL COLLEGE COST?

OK. You have made an estimate of your family contribution. Now you need to know how much it will cost to attend the college of your choice.

College costs and tuition are not synonymous. College costs—also known as "Cost of Attendance" or "Student Expense Budget"—are an aggregate of six elements.

1. **Tuition and fees** are the same for all attendees. They are paid to the college.
2. **Book and supply** expenditures depend on the courses you select. You can purchase these items in the college store, in the community, or you can save some money and buy them in a used book emporium.
3. **Housing** charges may vary depending upon where you choose to live; in a dorm, off-campus in an apartment, or at home, in your old room.
4. **Meal** charges can also vary. There is one figure if purchase a school meal plan. There is another figure if you plan to cook for yourself (usual translation: pasta, pizza, tunafish, and fast food). And there is still a third figure if you're enjoying home-cooked meals—it makes no difference how much this arrangement might add to your parents' normal costs.
5. **Personal expenses** represent all the money you spend at places other than the college. This includes upkeep of clothing, health insurance, even a small allowance for CDs, pizzas, and an occasional night out. The personal expense category can be very flexible. If you are handicapped, for instance, or have child care bills to shoulder, this item can be set very high.
6. **Transportation**, too, is flexible. It may be based on two or three roundtrips (economy class) between a distant campus and home or it may represent commuting expenses.

Expense budgets are established by the financial aid officer for the different categories of students who attend a typical college. There may be a separate budget for dependent students living in the dorm, dependent students in an apartment, dependent students who live at home, independent students in each of these categories, and subcategories for single and married independent students. In addition, the financial aid officer will make special allowances in the budget for the unique problems of the handicapped.

To illustrate this variety, note the different budgets established by one private college in California.

Student Category	Budget
Single Student, Lives at Home	$6,740
Single Student, Lives in Dorm	$11,770
Single Student, Lives in Own Apartment	$13,280
Married Student, Child Care Expenses	$17,600

Here are some points to ponder about expense budgets:

- Some items in the expense budget, such as room and board when you live at home, may not represent a special outlay for your family.
- By being frugal, your actual expenditures may be less than the college has allowed.
- If some of your college-related expenses do not appear to be accurately reflected in the expense budget, let the financial aid officer know. Any increase in the expense budget increases your eligibility for financial aid.

You can get excellent estimates of college costs from two handy references: The current editions of the College Board's *The College Cost Book* or the ACT's *College Planning/Search Book*. (See your guidance counselor). Of course, you will want to augment this information by writing directly to colleges and asking for their most current catalogue. Also remember, if the information you're using is for the 1991/92 year, and you aren't starting college until 1992/93, you should add about 8% to the total cost figure to get a better idea of the rate you'll be paying.

To get a quick idea of the relationship between your family contribution and college costs, we have developed a cost-of-attendance table for different types of institutions, projected to 1995/96. We have assumed a 7% annual increase in the cost of public schools and an 8% annual increase at the privates. Note that in a four-year, private college, your senior year could, conceivably, cost $4,555 more that your freshman year.

Type of Institution	1992/93 Resident	1992/93 Commuter	1993/94 Resident	1993/94 Commuter	1994/95 Resident	1994/95 Commuter	1995/96 Resident	1995/96 Commuter
4-Year Private	$17,540	$15,080	$18,940	$16,290	$20,450	$17,590	$22,095	$18,990
2-Year Private	11,740	9,400	12,680	10,150	13,700	10,960	14,790	11,840
4-Year Public	8,000	6,400	8,560	6,850	9,160	7,330	9,800	7,840
2-Year Public	7,040	5,330	7,530	5,700	8,060	6,100	8,625	6,530

QUESTION #3: WHAT'S MY NEED?

Now you have all the materials you need to answer the third question: How much need will I have at each college of my choice? You do that by comparing your Family Contribution, as determined from Appendix 1, 2, or 3, with the Cost of Attendance (all six elements) at each school that interests you.

MARCHING DOWN THE NEED-BASED ROUTE

Now that the first element in taking charge has been accomplished (Knowing the Money Numbers Ahead of Time), you can initiate the second element: Executing the Mechanics of the Application Process With Speed and Precision.

You submit your financial aid application form as soon after the first of the year as possible. We say "as soon after" because a great many programs unlocked by the form are time-sensitive. They operate on a first-come, first-served basis.

Which form should you fill out? That's up to the college or your state. Be sure to find out before January 1. If the schools to which you apply ask you to use different forms, before you spend the time on multiple applications, ask the FAOs about transferring data—it's very easy to have the information from the *Federal* portion of one application sent to other schools of your choice. Just send a letter to Processor #2 and request a duplicate Student Aid Report—Processor #2 can get any information it needs about you from the gigantic computer in the sky that processes all the federal aid eligibility data. Note: some schools may still ask you to provide supplemental information, in which case, you'll have to complete that part of the second form.

Agencies, Forms and Programs

| | | Purpose ||
Form	Sponsor	First-Come, First-Served Programs	Programs Not Time Sensitive
Application for Federal Student Aid (*AFSA*)	Federal Government	Federal Campus-Based Programs Some State Programs	Pell Grant
Family Financial Statement (*FFS*)	American College Testing Program	Federal Campus-Based Programs College's Own Resources Many State Programs Some Private Programs	Pell Grant Stafford Loans SLS Loans
Financial Aid Form (*FAF*)	College Scholarship Program	^	^
SingleFile	United Student Aid Funds	^	^
PHEAA Form	Pennsylvania Higher Education Assistance Agency	Same as above Pennsylvania State Grant	Same as above

Where do you get the forms? From your guidance office or any college financial aid office. The Table of Agencies, Forms and Programs lists the most widely used aid application forms, and indicates the programs they serve and which are first-come, first served.

HERE ARE SOME IMPORTANT POINTS

- **Social Security Number.** You must have a social security number to apply for financial aid. If you don't have one, get one in a hurry.
- **January 1.** Financial aid forms cannot be dated or submitted before January 1.
- **Date Due.** Be sure you know when colleges want you to submit the forms. If you apply to six colleges and each has a different date, make a list of these dates, and submit the form by the earliest of the dates on your list. The form, incidentally, goes to the colleges via the need analysis processor, so allow plenty of time.
- **Estimating Information.** If the earliest date falls before your mom and dad have done their income taxes, you can use estimates for the income and tax information that you must enter on the form.
- **Estimates That Are Not in the Ball Park.** If you note, later on, that your estimates were way off (outside a $200-$300 tolerance range), provide corrections to the need analysis services.
- **Comparison Between Need Analysis Forms and IRS Forms.** College financial aid officers must validate 30% of all financial aid forms, which means comparing the data with that found on your income tax return. This enormous amount of paperwork can delay the distribution of money to students. It also means that if you estimated the information, and were outside the tolerance range, and did not provide any corrections, the college will know and you will be asked to make corrections. Uncle Sam will pick over one million applications for validation. Accept the fact that tax returns and financial aid forms must

match rather closely, and be consistent. Clarence Shoemaker, the Director of Student Financial Aid at the University of South Dakota, has prepared a chart of those items on the FAF and FFS which must match with the information on your 1040. In addition to income, income tax paid and number of exemptions, these categories include the amount of your itemized deductions, payments to IRA, Keogh and 401(k) plans, Social Security Benefits, Medical and Dental Expenses not covered by insurance, and "other income" (for example, capital gains, alimony received, unemployment compensation, business income, tax-exempt income, earned income credit, and pensions and annuities).

- **A Good Use of the Winter Holiday.** On a quiet day, switch off the TV, sit down with your family, an income tax form and a financial aid application, and put red circles around these common items. At that time, you may wish to complete an estimated tax return so you can get a headstart on filling out the financial aid form.
- **College Financial Aid Forms.** Many colleges will ask you to submit their own forms in addition to the major aid forms listed in the table above. These go directly to the colleges and, thank the Heavens, are usually much simpler to fill out.
- **Change in Status.** If, after you have submitted your financial aid form, there is a change in your status (a family death, disability, prolonged unemployment, divorce or separation), notify the need analysis service.
- **Early Bird Gets the Worm.** Apply for financial assistance as early as possible. Schools can often meet the needs of the first applicants, and then run out of assistance money for the late applicants. The following extract from a letter originating in a college's financial aid office is typical:
   "...The University of X has not been able to meet the financial needs of all students in 1992/93. We are likely to be in this position again during the 1993/94 academic year and late financial aid applicants are likely to be affected."
- **Don't Make Mistakes** when filling out your financial aid applications. Mistakes cause the form to bounce. By the time you make corrections and resubmit it, you will find yourself at the end of the line and the money gone. Most common mistakes: Omitting social security number, forgetting to sign the form, leaving questions blank when you really mean zero, (write "0"), using "white-out," entering a range of figures such as $200-400, giving monthly amounts instead of yearly amounts or vice versa (read the question carefully to learn what information is required), entering cents, using a felt-tip pen (some processors require applicants to use a No. 2 pencil, even for their signatures), and writing illegibly.
- **Don't Falsify Anything.** As the top of the financial aid application clearly states, "If you purposely give false or misleading information on your form, you may be subject to a fine of $10,000, receive a prison sentence or both." And don't expect the financial planner you hired to bail you out.
- **Apply for a Pell Grant,** even if you know you aren't eligible. All it takes is checking off one box in the common aid applications. You must apply for a Pell to be eligible for other aid programs (including the Stafford Student Loan and the SLS Loan).
- **Make Copies** of all financial aid forms and your responses to requests for added information that may come to you from Uncle Sam, the need analysis processor, or the colleges. After making copies, consider using registered mail, return receipt requested. The College Board says this slows down processing, but Type A personalities may sleep better knowing their applications reached their proper destination.
- **If You are Male, Register for Selective Service.** You will not be eligible for financial aid unless you do. If you are exempt from registering for the draft, you must file a statement accordingly. This decision was upheld by a U.S. Appeals Court.
- **Most Importantly,** don't forget to include the processing fee.

WHAT HAPPENS NOW?

Your financial aid application is sent to the need analysis service. The service checks the information. If there is something wrong, the service will contact you. If there is nothing wrong, the service will convert your information into a Family Contribution. The service will also provide your information to Uncle Sam's Pell Grant processor, if you so direct and you should.

And finally, the service can determine your eligibility for a state grant. A summary of all these results is sent to you. A more detailed analysis is sent to the colleges you named.

Note: The Pell Grant eligibility (or ineligibility) report is called a Student Aid Report. Beginning with the 1990/91 award year, it became part of the report sent to you by the need analysis service rather than a separate document that came from Uncle Sam. It is still the student's responsibility to forward the report to any college he or she still plans to attend.

The college, meanwhile, will have learned from the need analysis service whether you are eligible for Pell and state grants and for how much. And, of course, it will have all your financial data as well as the calculated family contribution.

The financial aid officer now rolls up the ol' sleeves and goes to work. First, the FAO must determine your student expense budget. Second, the FAO reviews your family contribution. About 35% of all financial aid officers will adjust the contribution—based on policies of their office (10% admit to increasing the family contribution; 25% say they lower it). Third, the FAO determines your need. And fourth, he or she sets out to meet this need by building you a Financial Aid Package.

THE FINANCIAL AID PACKAGE

The bottom layer of the package is any assistance you may get from the federal Pell Grant program (see Chapter 10) and your state's student aid program (see Chapter 11).

Next, the financial aid officer draws on three major federal programs which are funded through colleges (see Chapter 10). They are the Carl D. Perkins Loan Program, the Supplemental Educational Opportunity Grant Program, and the College Work-Study Program. There are also some smaller specialized federal programs that can be tapped.

The next layer is taken from the college's own resources—special loan programs, unrestricted scholarships or restricted scholarships for which you may qualify. The richer the college, the more resources it will have for this layer in the package.

When awarding money from programs they administer but do not fund (i.e., some of the federal programs), colleges tend to give priority to the neediest of the able. When awarding money from their own funds, colleges tend to give priority to the ablest of the needy.

Next, the college will incorporate any scholarships you found on your own into the package.

If, after all this packaging, you still have need, the financial aid officer will recommend that you obtain a Stafford Student Loan (see Chapter 10). The size of your loan depends on your ability to pass a "remaining need" test. Remaining need, you will recall, equals Cost of Attendance less the Family Contribution and other student aid received.

THE AWARD LETTER

The financial aid package will be presented to you in the form of an award letter.

The award letter should contain three substantive and two administrative elements.

The substantive elements are (1) a statement of the expense budget developed for you; (2) your family contribution; and (3) the amount of your need, to include how all or part of that need is to be met, listing each aid source and dollar amount.

The administrative elements contain (1) a suspense date by which you must return the award letter and (2) information on available procedures for "appealing" any information in the award letter with which you disagree.

Compare the award letters you receive from all the colleges to which you applied. But don't delay responding to an award letter because you are still waiting for letters from other colleges. If you don't reply by the required date, your award will be cancelled (colleges can't hold money). Responding to the award letter does not commit you to attendance. It just safeguards your award, should you elect to go to that college. In responding to the award letter, you can accept the award in its entirety, accept some components of the award and reject others, reject the award entirely, or request a revision in the composition of awards (more grants, less loans).

Your success in appealing an award depends on a great number of factors; your timing, whether the college does or does not have discretionary funds, how badly the college wants you, how skillful and diplomatic you are in presenting your case, changes in your family situation of which the financial aid officer was unaware, etc. You should not enter this phase of the financial aid process without first reading our publication *Financial Aid Officers: What They Do—To You and For You* (See inside back cover).

WILL THE NEED-BASED ROUTE SATISFY MY NEED?

Maybe. Maybe not. If it does, it could be a dream package. But, it could also be an offer that leaves you several hundred or thousand dollars short or one that mires you deeply in debt. Remember:

- The fact that you have need does not necessarily mean your family's income qualifies for all assistance programs. Many programs have income ceilings.
- The college may not have enough resources to help all applicants.
- Different colleges may assess your need differently. If you apply to three schools, each of which costs $3,000 more than your family's assessed contribution, you may be offered three very different packages, ranging from the attractive to the unacceptable.

The point that cannot be stressed enough is that you should march down the need-based route. Don't consider yourself too rich or be too proud to ask for help. Take the required steps along the need-based route and take them with care and precision.

This brings us to the third element of the take-charge process: Knowing where the influence points are.

Influence Point	What You Can Gain	More Information
College Selection	Improved financial aid package, i.e., more grants than loans. No-need scholarships	Chapter 9
Preparing for Need-Analysis	A lowered family contribution and increased eligibility for aid. Longer planning time for help with cash-flow requirements	This Chapter, Chapter 7, Appendices 1, 2 and 3
Speed and Accuracy in Applying	Increased chance of tapping into limited aid sources	This Chapter
Dealing with Financial Aid Officers	Improved financial aid package.	This Chapter, Chapter 7, Chapter 9

A Final Word to the Wise. There is more money in being an informed consumer and taking charge of the aid link-up process than in all the scholarship hunts ever conducted!

Part III
Advanced Moves in Financial Aid

Chapter 7
For the Short Range: Tilting Things Your Way

NO-NEED AWARDS

No-need awards are scholarships given with no regard to your financial need. If you win a $2,000, no-need academic scholarship, you are $2,000 ahead.

The recipient of a no-need scholarship can fall into one of two categories with regard to college costs: 1. Has need; 2. Doesn't have need. Let's examine each situation in more detail:

Situation #1. **You have need and receive a no-need award.** The cost of college is then reduced by the amount of your award. This reduction may eliminate (1) part of your need; (2) your entire need; (3) your entire need and part of your family contribution; or (4) part of your family contribution, leaving your need intact.

Actual numbers and the policies of the college will determine which of these it will be. Assume the cost of college is $8,000 and your family contribution is $5,000. This makes your need $3,000. Example 1—Your no-need award is $1,000. Offered aid package: Your family contribution remains at $5,000; your need is reduced from $3,000 to $2,000. Example 2—Your no-need award is $3,000. Offered aid package: Your family contribution remains $5,000; your need is wiped out. Example 3—Your no-need award is $4,000. Offered aid package: Now your family contribution is reduced from $5,000 to $4,000; your need is wiped out. Example 4—Your no-need award is again $4,000, however, this college has a different packaging philosophy. It eliminates all but $1,000 of your family contribution, and leaves you with $3,000 in need.

Situation #2. **You have no need and the award is a no-need award.** In this case, the money goes directly to you. It replaces your money. You write a smaller check when you pay the college bill. Let's assign numbers to this. Your family contribution is $8,000 and the cost of college is $8,000; Example 1—Your no-need award is $3,000. Your family contribution shrinks to $5,000. That's all you have to pay. Example 2—Your no-need award is $10,000. You are now $2,000 ahead which will finance your winter vacation on the Amalfi Coast. Right? Wrong. You can only receive $8,000—the amount that eliminates your family contribution. Tuition aid of any kind, need based or not, cannot exceed the cost of attendance. Financial aid, in other words, cannot produce income for you.

Question. These no-need awards sound great. Where can I find one?
Answer. They tend to congregate in three areas.

1. **Uncle Sam.** The Federal government has two types of no-need awards. The first is for outstanding students as defined by each individual state (for example, The Robert C. Byrd Honors Scholarship Program—See Chapter 11). The second has a military connection and carries a service obligation. Good examples: the service academies, ROTC scholarships. See Chapter 13.
2. **The States.** Two types of programs. One—honor scholarships for outstanding students. Two—tuition equalization grants for in-state students who attend a private college rather than a public university. Both programs usually require students to remain in their home state. See Chapter 11 to learn whether your state operates either program.
3. **The Colleges.** Colleges are the main source of no-need awards. Most are academic scholarships designed to entice bright students to enroll at the sponsoring institution. See Chapter 9, 18, and *The A's and B's of Academic Scholarships* (inside back cover).

LESSONS FROM THE APPENDICES

We assume that while reading Chapter 6 you took the time to complete the worksheets in Appendix 1, 2, or 3 to estimate your family contribution. These are the items that should have caught your eye.

1. **Asset Assessment Rates.** A dependent student does not rate an asset protection allowance. The dependent student's assets are taxed at 35% of their value. Parents do rate an asset protection allowance. Money held by parents, as you trace it through the formula, is taxed about 5.6%. That's quite a difference! $35,000 in junior's bank account becomes a $12,250 contribution to college costs. The same $35,000 in the parental account becomes a mere $1,960 contribution. Lesson: Accumulate money for college, yes. But don't be so quick to accumulate in the child's name.

2. **The True Value of a Student Aid Dollar.** If you are in a 28% tax bracket and don't get student aid, you must earn $1.39 to have one dollar available for tuition bills. Let's turn this around. If you are successful in getting one dollar of student aid, that one dollar is really worth $1.39 to you. Lesson: The higher your tax bracket, the greater the value of any student aid dollar received.

3. **The Previous Year Rule.** Your 1991 calendar year earnings determine your aid eligibility for the 1992/93 academic year. Your 1992 earnings impact on the 1993/94 school year. If your income fluctuates, and you have some control over the fluctuations, you might wish to defer income from the base year to the next. That would enhance your eligibility in the coming academic year. What about the next base year? Life is filled with soap opera twists. Take it one year at a time.

4. **Federal Income Tax Versus Student Aid Eligibility.** Federal income taxes (and state income taxes which normally swim in the wake of the federal tax) have a distinct relationship to student aid eligibility. Pay more in taxes and your aid eligibility increases; pay less in taxes and your aid eligibility decreases. You may want to keep this relationship in mind before you engage in tax reduction schemes such as buying into a tax shelter or making a large donation to a charity. For a family whose adjusted available income (Line 24 in Appendix 1) is over $18,700 per year (and assuming state income taxes weigh in at approximately 20% of the federal tax burden), each additional tax dollar paid will increase aid eligibility by $0.57; each tax dollar saved will reduce aid eligibility by $0.57.

Question. Why are you telling me all this? How can I take advantage of this knowledge?
Answer. It's all in the numbers. Suppose that by working the appendices you determine you will have $450 of need at College A, your first choice school. A $450 need may qualify you for a Stafford Student Loan but finding a lender for a loan under $500 will be very difficult. Now, through an accounting maneuver, you manage to increase your combined federal and state taxes by $130. What happens? Your need will grow from $450 to $524. A need of $524 makes finding a lender easy. That is $524 your parents won't have to cover with a check. Even after paying $130 more in taxes, their checking balance will be $394 ahead.

5. **Business Property.** Assets held by an individual are taxed on a dollar for dollar basis. Assets that are part of a business rate an adjustment factor (e.g., 40% of net worth up to $75,000) Think hard. Do you have any source of income, from a hobby or property or whatever, that you can treat as a business? Or can you shift assets to a sub-S corporation in which your family holds a controlling 51% interest while people outside the need analysis formula (your grandmother?) hold 49%? That's a real one-two punch. Not only do you get the asset value reduced by the net worth adjustment, but there is a second reduction stemming from the 49% value transfer outside the immediate family. All this will make your tax return more complex, but the trade-off is a sharply reduced contribution to college costs.

6. **Consumer Debt.** Under the need analysis formula, you get no credit for consumer debt. If you owe the bank $15,000 in car payments, that's your problem. But let's say you establish a special account that lets you borrow against your home equity (the present value of your home minus what you still owe on it). If you draw $15,000 from this account to buy the new car, you have in effect reduced your home equity—a reportable item—by that

amount. You pay less for college and have a new car to boot! An added benefit, under tax reform, interest payments on consumer debt are no longer deductible, while interest payments on equity credit lines are. By using a home equity to finance your car purchase, you have reduced your assets for need analysis while making sure the interest on your car payments is still deductible

TILTING THINGS YOUR WAY

There are five strategies available for tilting the financial aid process in your favor. Only two of the strategies are mutually exclusive. The Napoleon of aid seekers would probably investigate all five.

STRATEGY 1—REDUCING THE FAMILY CONTRIBUTION

In the chart on your left, A is your family contribution. B stands for your need. And C is the cost of attendance at the college of your choice.

Objective: Reduce A (your contribution) so that B (your need) becomes larger. In other words, make yourself eligible for more student assistance.

Methods:

1. **Thoroughly understand the need analysis process,** the factors considered, the percentages and weights assigned to the data. Determine whether you can make adjustments in your situation so that you will be treated in a way that is more advantageous to you.
2. **Reduce the value of assets you report for need analysis (I).** Under "Lessons From the Appendices" we talked about why parental assets count less than student assets. We talked about how certain loans can be used to reduce assets. And we talked about the possibilities of shifting assets to "sole proprietorships" or corporations. But there is more.
3. **Reduce the value of your assets (II).** How? Example: Do you know the true value of your home? Assessed values (which reflect recent sales prices) can become distorted through the use of "creative financing"—a technique that balances smaller monthly payments by buyers, often far below going interest rates, with an artificial increase in the home's valuation. Operating in exactly the opposite direction was a Supreme Court decision that limited the right of sellers to pass on to buyers an original, low-interest mortgage. This decision tends to lower the prices of homes. Our advice: Take a hard look at what your home is really worth before you fill in a need analysis form. One caution: Report your home's present value accurately. The need analysis computer will take the original purchase price and compound it by a multiplier derived exclusively for the purpose of need analysis. To win your "Computers Adore Honesty" button, your statement of home value should exceed this computer calculation. If it doesn't, you will be asked questions.
4. **Reduce the value of your assets (III).** Do you need to make a large purchase before you sign and date your need analysis form? We've already suggested purchasing a car. How about a new stereo, refrigerator or washer-dryer? Pay cash for the purchase, if you can. That will substantially reduce your reportable assets—and provide you with good music, some cold drinks and a few clean clothes.
5. **Use the student's assets first.** If you have been saving money in your child's name, get his or her permission to use that money to pay your entire family contribution for the first year of college. This will improve your chances for financial aid during years two, three, and four.
6. **Declare yourself independent.** Obviously, independent (or self-supporting) students do not include their parents' income and assets in their need analysis calculation; only their own, more limited resources. Hence, their contribution will generally be smaller, and their need larger.

Should you declare yourself independent then, to gain access to more aid? Certainly, if you are really independent and can meet the test for independence described in Chapter 4. Absolutely not, if it is a ploy. Now review the golden words in Chapter 4 dealing with dependent and independent students.

7. **Use the most favorable need analysis method.** For families with incomes under $15,000, make sure you estimate your family contribution under the full-data Congressional Methodology and the simplified Congressional Methodology. Some might benefit by NOT taking advantage of Uncle Sam's simplified need test, especially families with low incomes, few assets, and high unreimbursed medical/dental expenses or secondary education tuitions. Be sure to have your financial aid application analyzed using both methods. The financial aid officer will then have a clearer picture of your financial situation as he or she puts together your financial aid package.
8. **Take less pay.** Is there any way for you to defer year-end bonuses? Remember, need analysis looks at previous year income—1991 for the 1992/93 award year. With reauthorization of the higher education laws looming ahead, who knows what the financial aid picture will look like for next year. If you can increase your eligibility even for a year, do it!
9. **Accelerate or postpone gains and losses.** If you plan to sell stocks or property, do it two years before college, or wait until your student has graduated. Realized gains count as income which is heavily "taxed" by the need analysis system.
10. **Start a family business.** It doesn't have to be complex. Some examples. The Bakers started Babycakes Inc. to sell muffins every Saturday morning at their local farmer's market. Rose loved going to yard sales on weekends, so, she started a second hand furniture business with the objects she found. Phil loved to buy the "mystery boxes" of stamps advertised in auction catalogues. He and his daughter would wash and sort the stamps, then resell them to other collectors. Uncle Sam rewards private enterprise with a greatly reduced expected contribution to college costs. If you're thinking about starting a larger business than the ones described above, reduce your assets further by using some of your home equity to cover the start up costs. Also remember, any money you pay your children becomes a business expense.
11. **Save for retirement.** Need analysis wants to know how much you contribute to a retirement account the year before college (it considers your contribution a discretionary item and adds that money back in to your total income). It does not, however, ask how much you've already saved. In other words, you can accumulate money tax-free (or tax-deferred) at the same time you reduce your assets for need analysis and save for your retirement. Please be aware, however, that some private colleges will ask about the value of your retirement funds and ask you to borrow against them. Also, you don't want all your assets tied up in funds that penalize you for early withdrawal (e.g., before age 59 1/2). You may need some money sooner.
12. **Go complex.** If you choose this option, be willing to pay a personal financial planner—one who really understands student aid (and such planners are not easy to find). Here is a gem from Marty Singer, CFP, a partner at Summit Financial Resources (354 Eisenhower Parkway, Livingston, New Jersey 07039, 201-992-8666)

"...The two key methods of increasing aid eligibility are to reduce Adjusted Gross Income and to move assets outside the view of the financial aid formulas. Employees of large companies have little chance to reduce formula income. If, however, you work for a small corporation, or if you are self-employed, you may be able to arrange a deferred compensation agreement where the employer reduces your salary in return for larger payments after the children are educated. Small business owners have great control over their reported earnings and can postpone income by reinvesting profits in business equipment, setting up a pension plan or creating their own deferred compensation program. Since the aid formulas favor business assets with a substantial protection allowance, it is advantageous to convert money that would otherwise be income into a business asset.

"For most middle-income families, the greatest opportunity to qualify for more financial aid comes from repositioning assets, by moving them outside the view of the formula. One way to do this is to mortgage your house to the hilt. Take the proceeds, most of your savings, and all of your child's money and redeploy them in tax-deferred investment vehicles. For example, nowhere does the financial aid form ask for the cash value of life insurance or deferred annuities. Your money will be safe and earn tax-deferred interest.

Of course, a careful cash flow analysis is essential. You will now have sizeable monthly mortgage payments in addition to your (reduced) contribution to college costs. But, by using a properly-structured universal life policy, you can keep your money out of the formula yet still have it readily available. Within limits, you may make tax-free withdrawals without penalty to provide yourself adequate cash flow to meet all your obligations. Amounts not needed during the college years may be invested in fixed or variable annuities to provide tax-deferred growth, investment balance and diversification.

"If the plan is set up properly, you may find yourself with a much lower family contribution, considerable income tax savings, a diversified investment program, and inexpensive life insurance paid for with untaxed dollars all at the same time. Warning: The value and features of insurance policies and contracts vary widely, and there are many complicated rules that must be followed to protect the tax-free status of insurance withdrawals.

"Strategies like the one just described have made it possible for parents to provide their children with the best education for which they qualify without breaking the family piggy bank. But you should not attempt to set up such a plan yourself. You will need to consult a knowledgeable professional to guide you through the many traps that await the inexperienced adventurer."

STRATEGY 2—INCREASING THE COST OF ATTENDANCE

In the chart on your left, A is your family contribution. B stands for your need. And C is the cost of attendance at the college of your choice.

Objective: Increase C (the cost of attendance) so B (your need) becomes larger. The technique is especially appropriate for the "remaining need" calculation that determines the size of a Stafford Student Loan.

Methods:

1. **Pick a more expensive school** if you assume there is a direct relationship between cost and quality of education. Example: Your family contribution is $5,000 and you plan to attend a $6,000 school. The maximum Stafford Loan for which you qualify is $1,000. If you now select a $7,500 school, you could qualify for a $2,500 loan. Remember, your family contribution does not change.

2. **Be sure all your expenses are reflected in the "Cost of Attendance."** Does the financial aid officer have a true picture of your transportation costs, special medical expenses, or other legitimate expenses that may have been overlooked by the school? Unfortunately, FAOs cannot include the cost of a new computer in your cost of attendance figure UNLESS the school explicitly requires all students to own one! Here, however, is a situation that can work! Your family contribution is $5,000 and the financial aid officer has established a $6,000 cost of attendance for you. The maximum Stafford Loan for which you can qualify is $1,000. You now convince the financial aid officer your budget must include $500 for physical therapy made necessary by a recent car accident. Your budget now becomes $6,500 and you qualify for a $1,500 Stafford Loan.

Now you try one. Unbeknownst to the financial aid officer (as well as the admission committee), one incoming student is a werewolf. What will be the student's extra expenses? Bars for the windows. Dead bolt locks. Paying for roomie to stay at the Holiday Inn during every full moon. An occasional sack of Purina dog chow. Flea collars. Rabies shots. City dog tags. A monthly shampoo and pedicure. You complete the list...

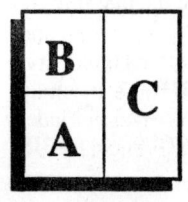

STRATEGY 3—OBTAINING AN IMPROVED AID PACKAGE

The aid package that covers your need—B—is loaded with loan money that, one day, you will have to repay. You don't like that.

Objective: Change the composition of the aid package to emphasize assistance that does not have to be repaid—grants and work-study opportunities.

Methods:
1. **Apply to colleges as early as possible,** before their money runs out.
2. **Pick a college where you are in the top 25% of the applicant pool.** The most desirable applicants get the most agreeable aid packages. That's as true at the Ivies as it is at Horned Toad State.
3. **If necessary, negotiate with the financial aid officer.** But remember, you can negotiate only if the college really wants you. What gives you bargaining strength? Good grades and high SATs, athletic ability, artistic talents, alumni ties, ethnic background, geographic origin—colleges like to brag the diversity of their student body, and they might be missing a pole vaulter from Idaho or a soprano from Rhode Island. You might even ask a department head (if you are a genius) or a coach (if you are a triple-threat) to be your ally and advocate in such negotiations.
4. **Find Scholarships.** Locate outside scholarships. These scholarships can improve your aid package if even part of their value is used to replace a loan element (and that decision rests with the FAO).

STRATEGY 4—REPLACING YOUR MONEY WITH OTHER PEOPLE'S MONEY

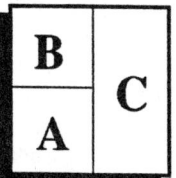

Objective: Getting somebody else's money to pay for A—your family contribution—is the most desirable but also the most difficult strategy. People often think that by finding a scholarship—any scholarship—they have replaced their own contribution. That, of course, is not so. The scholarship usually finds its way into the B box.

Method:
Qualify for a "no-need" scholarship. See opening section of this chapter.

STRATEGY 5—LOWERING THE COST OF COLLEGE

Attempt to lower the cost of college—C—so as to reduce or eliminate your need—B.

Objective: To avoid going through the hassle of applying for aid or saddling yourself with debt following graduation.

Methods:
1. **Pick a lower-priced school** such as one in an area where the cost of living is low (e.g., Texas, Oklahoma, Michigan) or one that receives church subsidies (e.g., Brigham Young, St. Olaf). And most importantly, don't overlook your own State U.
2. **Examine each of the six elements that make up "cost of attendance"** at a college. Some are firmly established (such as tuition), but others can be influenced. For example, used books cost a lot less than new ones!
3. **Accelerate college** by taking college courses for credit while in high school or by getting credit on advanced placement examinations. Hundreds of our nation's schools (including Harvard) will grant students sophomore standing. Each credit hour you pick up can be worth as much as $300 (depending on the college's tuition costs).
4. **Go to a community college for two years,** then transfer to a four-year school to finish your degree. You pick up the "halo" of the prestige college's sheepskin, but at a fraction of the cost.
5. **Investigate external degree programs.** Take correspondence courses, or study at home. Regents College seems the most comprehensive. For course and program information, write Regents College Degrees, Cultural Education Center, Albany, NY, 12230.

Another option worth investigating is education through public television. Many stations have agreements with colleges to offer courses for credit. Mind Extension University, in conjunction with Colorado State University, Washington State University, and the University of Minnesota, lets cable subscribers get course credit at home, that may later be applied toward degree programs at most colleges. Sample courses include: Analytical Geometry and Calculus; Family Relationships; Conversational French; the US

Constitution; and Economics (Macro- and Micro-). Call 1-800-777-MIND for tuition and registration information. An even larger program is the Public Broadcasting System's Adult Learning Service. These telecourses are accepted for credit at over 1500 colleges and enrollment has topped the 1.3 million mark. WARNING: Make sure you check the accreditation for all of these programs. Non-accredited courses will not count toward a degree.

6. **Get credit for life experience.** Different schools have their own rules on what experiences count for what credit. The American Council on Education publishes guidelines in a book called The National Guide to Educational Credit for Training Programs. Another option is to take the College Board's College-Level Examination Program (CLEP) Test.

The best summary of all these options is *Bear's Guide to Earning Non-Traditional Degrees*, which is available for $11.95 from Ten Speed Press, PO Box 7123, Berkeley, CA 94707.

HELP WITH THE CASH FLOW

Your family contribution must be paid each semester. For some people, the contribution can be as small as the "student earnings" which colleges assess almost automatically, regardless of whether you actually found a job.

For those who have assembled vast quantities of worldly goods, the family contribution can represent a rather sizable sum that usually comes with a friendly note "unless this bill is paid by such and such a date your student will not be allowed to register for classes..."

How can you pay this bill without selling the family home, jeopardizing your after-retirement financial security or taking out a high-cost commercial loan? One could turn to Uncle Sam and his PLUS/SLS Loan program (see Chapter 10). But PLUS/SLS Loans have some drawbacks. One, payments start within 60 days of taking out the loan. Two, they offer little flexibility in repayment. And, three, they have the usual comet's tail of paperwork, special forms, certifications, back-and-forth mailings, and other rigmarole usually attached to federal programs.

Objective: To pay your family contribution without liquidating assets, hocking the family jewels, or playing Uncle Sam's paper games.

Methods:

1. **Select a college that offers favorable, middle-income loan programs,** either from its own endowment funds or through money raised by state tax-exempt bond issues (more on these in Chapter 9).
2. **Select a college that permits you to pay the family contribution in installments** (Chapter 9).
3. **Participate in a commercial college tuition payment plan.** Here is how some plans work: You predetermine your cash requirement for college—say $2,000 at the start of each semester. The commercial organization makes that lump sum payment to the college when it is due. You, in turn, make monthly payments to the commercial organization. Frequently, the plans have a life insurance feature that covers bills in the event of your death or total disability. If the account with the commercial organization is in your favor, you are paid interest. If the account has a negative balance you pay the interest. Sponsors of this, and tuition credit line plans include the Knight Insurance Agency, 800-225-6783; EFI Fund Management, 2700 Sanders Rd., Prospect Heights, IL 60070 (available only at schools that have adopted the service; check with your college's financial aid office); Academic Management Services, 50 Vision Blvd., PO Box 14608, East Providence, RI 02914, 800-635-0120; The Tuition Plan, 57 Regional Dr., Concord, NH 03301, 800-822-8764; Collegeaire, PO Box 88370, Atlanta, GA 30356, 404-952-2500; Tuition Management Systems, Box 335, Newport, RI, 02840, 800-722-4867; and The Education Credit Line, National Educational Financial Services Corporation, 501 Silverside Road, Suite 125, Wilmington, DE 19809, 800-477-4977.

Be sure to compare plans before you sign on any dotted lines. Finance charges can vary greatly, as can the repayment schedules. Our examination of brochures found Collegeaire to have the lowest overall cost as well as the greatest flexibility, but again, we advise you to do some checking on your own.

4. **Borrow from a commercial loan source.** Here are four of the largest educational lenders/guarantors. **TERI.** Loans of up to $20,000 per year with 20 years to repay. Repayment begins 45 days after the college receives the loan money (although families may defer paying back the principal for up to 4 years while the student is enrolled). Other costs consist of a guarantee fee equal to 5% of the total loan amount. The interest rate equals the prime rate plus 1-2%. Contact The Education Resource Institute, 330 Stuart Street, Suite 500, Boston, MA 02116, 1-800-255-TERI. This plan comes under a variety of other names (for example, VALUE and Alliance) depending on the plan's co-sponsor. TERI acts as the guarantor. **NELLIE MAE.** The New England Education Loan Marketing Corporation offers similar loans (EXCEL and SHARE), but with a few exceptions. Most importantly, SHARE and EXCEL may be secured with a home mortgage, which means the interest payments could be tax-deductible. For more information, write Nellie Mae, 50 Braintree Hill Park, Suite 300, Braintree, MA 02184, 800-634-9308 (in MA, 617-849-3447). **SALLIE MAE.** The Student Loan Marketing Association offers a wide variety of programs for both graduate and undergraduate students. For example, using an Extra Credit Loan, you can borrow up to $10,000 per year at an interest rate equal to the bond equivalent of the 91-day T-bill plus 4%. For more information, write SALLIE MAE, 1050 Thomas Jefferson Street, NW, Washington, DC 20007, 800-874-9390. **ConSern.** Loans of up to $15,000 per year with 12 years to repay. Repayment begins 30 days after the student receives the loan money (although families may defer paying back the principal for up to four years while the student is enrolled). Other costs consist of an application fee of $55 and a discount fee equal to 4% of the total loan amount. The interest rate is adjusted monthly an equals the 3-month commercial paper note rate plus 4.1%. Contact ConSern, 205 Van Buren St. #200, Herndon, VA 22070, 800-767-5626 or 703-709-5626.
5. **Tap your home equity.** If your family has a good income and credit history, you can borrow up to 80% of the market value of your home minus the outstanding balance of your mortgage. In other words, if you own a $100,000 home and have $30,000 remaining on the mortgage, you can borrow up to $50,000 (calculation:[100,000 X .8]-30,000). There is a small fee to open the account, but after that, you can borrow whatever amount you need, whenever you need it, without ever having to reapply. To use the funds, you simply write a check or use a credit card. Interest rates float about two percentage points above the prime. And here's an added bonus. Any items you charge against your credit line—like college tuition—will become part of your home mortgage. Your assets are reduced for purposes of need analysis, and your interest payments on loans up to $100,000 become tax-deductible (unless the proceeds are used to buy annuities or tax-exempt bonds). Home equity loans are an extremely easy and flexible way to obtain cash flow assistance on favorable terms. But care must be taken that the ease of access to all this money will not result in deep financial problems and cause you to lose your home. The total monthly payments on all of your loans should not exceed 35% of your pre-tax monthly income.

    Here are some questions to ask before you take out a home equity loan: What is the initial rate of interest? If it's variable, how often can the rate change? On what index is it based? Does it carry a cap? Is there an annual fee? An application fee? An origination fee? Can any of the terms be changed without my approval? Under what circumstances can the bank require repayment of the outstanding credit?
6. **Borrow against your pension plan.** If you participate in a company pension or profit-sharing plan, you may be able to borrow against the equity built up in it. Or, if you are a self-employed professional with a retirement plan, you can do some borrowing. Under tax reform, you can borrow half the amount you have vested up to $50,000, less your highest loan balance during the preceding 12 months. The interest rate hovers around the prime and the money must be repaid within five years. Employers may impose additional regulations.
7. **Draw out some of the money accumulated in an IRA account.** You'll probably be hit with a 10% penalty and a bill from the IRS, so, if you need $6,000, draw out a little extra to take care of both the bursar and Uncle Sam. As usual, there is an exception. This time it's found in Section 72(t)(2)(A)(iv) of the tax code (or so I'm told). You can escape the

tax collector and withdraw funds before you turn 59 1/2, provided you receive the money in equal, periodic payments extending over the rest of your years.

"WHAT IF" CALCULATIONS

Every sophisticated family should try a few "what if" situations, using the Appendix 1, 2, or 3 family contribution worksheets. If you have a home computer with spreadsheet software like Excel or LOTUS 1-2-3, these appendices are easily programmed, and make "what-if" calculations simple. Another option is to order our software package (see inside back cover). The results can surprise you. Here are a few "what-if" suggestions.
1. How does a charitable gift of $1,000 or $2,000 impact on our family contribution?
2. Should Mom get a job to help with college costs?
3. If Dad needs to complete his degree to work, is there any advantage to his returning to school at the same time one or more children are in college?
4. If you have two children, one year apart, with one starting college and one starting the senior year in high school, would it be advantageous for the older child to "stop out" for one year and wait for son or daughter #2 to catch up?
5. Do grandparents need some extra money? You can each give each of your student's grandparents a gift of up to $10,000. That could reduce your assets by as much as $80,000. It could also reduce the amount of tax being paid, as frequently, grandparents are retired and in a lower tax bracket.
6. Can you shift some assets into a business venture?
7. What happens if you make a large purchase, such as a car, and pay cash or use an equity line of credit?
8. Try some "what-ifs" of your own.

WHAT PEOPLE WON'T TRY

1. **Students buy campus property.** Linda Wallace, a University of Wisconsin student, purchased a condominium near the campus for $60,000. When she graduated, she sold it for a $30,000 profit—enough to pay off four years of college expenses.

    Becky and Louis James moved to San Diego to attend the University of California. They bought a three-bedroom house, converted a shed into a fourth bedroom, and collected rent from roommates. The James' are tickled pink with their investment. The rent covers mortgage payments. And, by owning property, the James' established California residency, saving each more than $1,000 a year in out-of-state tuition.

    Of course, Linda and the James' also saved on college room and board charges.

2. **Mom and Dad buy campus rental property.** This takes a more sophisticated approach. Not only do you get the benefits of annual deductions for mortgage interest, operating expenses and depreciation, but your college student offspring can receive a steady salary while in school; a salary you may deduct as a business expense. How? By having that son or daughter live in one of the units and draw pay from you as residential property manager. At the same time, he or she saves on room and board. In addition, your campus visits can be written off, because, as far as the tax collector is concerned, the purpose of the trip is to inspect the condition of your property. And, if your real estate appreciates, you can sell the property and pocket the after tax share of the capital gain. There is still one more advantage. If you purchase the property (or make a down payment on the property) with funds that used to be personal assets, you have moved them into the business category which provides you with a net worth adjustment in the need analysis formula.

    To take advantage of all this, be sure your property qualifies as rental property (and not personal property). In other words, Mom or Dad cannot use it for more than 14 days or 10% of the total days they rent it out. Here's why. In an effort to eliminate tax shelters, Uncle Sam and the IRS now distinguish between the treatment of personal property and the treatment of rental property. The IRS limits deductible losses from the rental of personal property to the amount of rental income received. The IRS places no such limit on losses from rental property, however, these losses may no longer be used to offset salary income.

They may only be used to offset what the IRS calls passive income—income from limited partnerships or other rental property. Furthermore, the IRS limits the deduction of mortgage interest to the amount allocated to rental use (if, however, the property is rented for 100% of the year, 100% of the mortgage interest may still be deducted). There is still some good news in all this. Families with AGIs under $100,000 who actively manage their property, may use up to $25,000 of real estate losses to shelter "nonpassive " (salary) income. NOTE: The IRS recently published 266 pages of rules on passive/active losses. We've tried to summarize it in the paragraphs above, but still suggest you speak with an accountant or tax attorney before you undertake this kind of venture.

3. Get on Mom or Dad's payroll. Can either of your parents give you a job in the family business? Your earnings become a tax deductible business expense. If you're under 18, you do not have to pay social security tax on your wages. And, if you can limit your earnings to under $3,400 per year ($5,400 if you contribute to an IRA), you will owe no federal income tax. Please note: The Congressional Methodology assesses student earnings at 70%, so $3,400 in after-tax wages turns into a $2,380 contribution to college costs.

4. Give a gift. An individual can make a $10,000 tax-free gift each year to another individual. A married couple can double that and make it a $20,000 gift. Under conventional wisdom, grandparents are the ones who usually take advantage of this tax wrinkle to help their smart grandchildren with college. Under unconventional wisdom, (as we explained under "what-ifs" to try) parents might consider making an annual gift to grandparents. The purpose: To reduce their own asset position for need analysis and pay less for college. The money, meanwhile, really did not leave the family. A gift of securities is especially advantageous. If they have appreciated, you avoid paying tax on the gain. And, if they continue to appreciate after they have been transferred, they can be inherited at this higher value, and still no one has had to pay tax on the gain.

6. Start an educational benefit trust. Small, closely held corporations can establish educational benefit trusts to pay the college expenses of employees' children—that means all employees—the president's as well as the maintenance crew's. The corporation makes regular payments to the trust. The trust, which is governed by a bank or attorney not connected with the corporation, then invests the funds which accumulate tax-free. Once an eligible person reaches college age, a predetermined amount of tuition money is withdrawn. This disbursement must be treated as a taxable benefit by the student's parents. Thus, the president who is in a higher bracket will probably gain less than a member of the maintenance crew.

7. Start a company scholarship program. This is not as complex as a trust. Still, the program must meet an IRS test to qualify as a business expense. The test usually involves a set of standards; beneficiaries must have a B average; their mother or father must have worked for the company at least five years; the plan is limited to employees with salaries under $50,000. A second part of the test deals with eligibility. All employees' children must be eligible. If the scholarships are limited to the children of corporate officers and directors, the company will flunk the test.

8. Borrow against a brokerage account. This is another way to avoid the "nondeductibility of consumer interest" feature of the tax laws. If the loan is used to buy investment property, interest is deductible up to the amount of investment income produced. We suggest you sell some securities to pay your college bills, then use a loan to buy more securities (Note: You can't deduct interest on a loan used to buy tax-exempt investments such as municipal bonds, because you don't pay tax on the resulting income from these bonds). If you do decide to borrow against your brokerage account (this is known as a margin loan), be very careful. Borrowing limits are usually 50% of the account value. If your margined security takes a tumble on the market, your broker will require more cash or collateral to maintain your loan. October 16, 1987. Need I say more?

Chapter 8
Long-Range Planning: College Is Still Years Away

COLLEGE IS STILL YEARS AWAY
When college is still years away, the name of the game is to accumulate enough money to help with the inevitable bills. Here are thirteen suggestions:
1. **Savings in the Parents' Name.** Interest earned will be taxed at your rate rather than the child's rate. But there is an overriding advantage we will discuss later. Some of the safest, and easiest ways for parents to save money are through short- and long-term CDs, money-market funds, Treasury bills (which mature in 13, 26 or 52 weeks), Treasury notes (which mature in 1 to 5 years), Treasury bonds (which mature in 10 to 30 years), and US savings bonds. EE bonds, one type of US savings bond, have added advantages that are described later on in this chapter. As you shop around for rates, remember brokerage firms usually offer the highest rates on CDs and money-market funds. Also remember, the most lucrative ways to save money are generally the riskiest.
2. **A Savings Account in Junior's Name.** As a result of tax-reform, this type of income shifting has lost much of its appeal. For children under 14, the first $550 in interest or dividend income is tax-free. The next $550 is taxed at the child's rate. And any unearned income in excess of $1,100 is taxed at the parents' rate. The solution? Take advantage of the fact that unearned income of children over 14 is still taxed at the child's rate. If you have young children, your gifts should take the form of tax-deferred investments, such as US Savings Bonds (see below) and fast growing stocks. Once the child reaches 14, redeem the bonds, sell the stocks, and place the proceeds in a safe, but high yielding investment. Another way to save in Junior's name is through the use of trusts, as described below.
3. **Uniform Gifts to Minors Act (UGMA).** An irrevocable gift to a child made via a "custodial account." The custodian is responsible for managing the funds until the minor reaches the age of majority. The money which accumulates does so under the minor's lower tax liability. UGMA has a few drawbacks. First, the amount of paperwork involved when the funds are finally transferred to the minor is enormous (a detailed accounting report is required). Second, once the funds are finally turned over, the child can do whatever he or she wants with them. Pay for college, pay for a new car, pay for a lifetime supply of jelly donuts...
4. **Establish a Minority Trust.** Under section 2503(c) of the tax code, families can establish an inter-vivos (living) trust for a minor, provided the funds are used solely for the benefit of that minor. This trust has two advantages over a UGMA. First, the trustee has control over the funds until the "donee" is 21 years old—well into the college paying years. Second, the trust pays its own income tax, thus avoiding the "age 14" kiddie tax rule. The first $3,450 in trust income is taxed at 15%; the next $6,900 is taxed at 28%; and anything above $10,350 is taxed at 31%.
5. **Establish a Crummey Trust.** Named for the court case under which it originated, this is very similar to the 2503(c) trust described above, but with one important exception. The recipient of the trust (presumably your child) may withdraw any contributions made to the trust in that year. If your child makes no withdrawals, the contribution is added to the principal. The trust may continue as long as the trustee chooses.

Individuals may each make a tax-free gift of up to $10,000 to either of these two trusts. The drawbacks? You'll need an attorney, and several hundred dollars to set up a trust and, you'll have to file separate income tax returns for them.

6. **Create a Charitable Remainder Unitrust.** You donate a set amount of money (usually at least $20,000) to a college or a charitable institution, such as your alma mater or the American Association of University Women, but stipulate that from 5% or 10% of the value of the gift, be paid out each year into a custodial account established for your college-bound student. At the end of a designated time frame, the principal goes to the college or charity. Meanwhile, you, the donor have (1) had a substantial tax deduction (2) built a college fund for junior and (3) given money to a favored charity. You'll need professional help to set up such a trust.
7. **Give a Gift.** An individual can make a $10,000 tax-free gift to another individual. A married couple can make a $20,000 gift. Grandparents are the ones who usually take advantage of this tax wrinkle to help their smart grandchildren through college. It can also help reduce any eventual estate taxes, if grandparents have a sizable estate.
8. **Invest in Government Bonds.** Parents who have purchased US EE savings bonds after January 1, 1990 will not have to pay any tax on the interest that accrues, provided the bonds are used to pay for their children's education. Full benefits are available to couples with incomes of $60,000 or less and to single parents with incomes of $40,000 or less when it's time to redeem their bonds. The exemption will taper off for families with incomes above these limits, and disappear completely for couples with incomes above $90,000 and single parents with incomes above $55,000. Income limitations will be indexed for inflation, so, by the time you redeem your bonds, the income ceilings may be much higher. One Catch: Your income for the year in which you plan to redeem your bonds includes all the interest the bonds have earned! This additional income may push some families right past the income cut-offs and ironically eliminate their exclusion! Bonds may be purchased at any time during the year, but the purchasers must be at least 24 years of age. In other words, families with incomes too high to benefit from the tax break may not have their children take advantage of the benefit by buying the bond themselves. For the same reason, grandparents and couples who file separate tax returns are also ineligible to participate. Families are guaranteed a rate of at least 6%, but as of this writing, yields are as high as 7.55%. Bonds are available through payroll deductions and at most banks and credit unions. For more information, write Office of Public Affairs, US Savings Bonds Division, Washington, DC 20226.
9. **A Savings Account Which Becomes a Line of Credit.** Build up savings in a Collegeaire Plan. By the time your children are in college, you will have a credit line that is 2 1/2 times as large as your savings account, with 81 months to pay it off. Your payments consist of a monthly principal payment and an interest charge on the outstanding balance of your credit account (not your total credit line). When your credit account is paid, your original savings, including interest earned, are returned to you in full. Here is an extract from the Collegeaire Table:

Yearly Amount You Need	Total Credit Line	Total Savings You Will Need	Minimum Monthly Repayment
$5,000	$20,000	$8,000	$246.92
$9,000	$36,000	$14,400	$444.45
$12,000	$48,000	$19,200	$592.59

Say you need $5,000 per year for 4 years of college. That translates into a $20,000 line of credit which requires an initial savings account balance of $8,000. Assuming you use the entire line of credit, you will make 81 monthly payments of $246.92 which totals $20,000. (Collegeaire, PO Box 88370, Atlanta, GA 30356. Phone: (404) 952-2500).
10. **Invest in Zero Coupon Bonds.** These are essentially municipal bonds, corporate bonds, and treasury bonds stripped of their interest coupons. Owners receive no income while

holding the bonds. Instead, the income is compounded semi-annually and re-invested. At some time in the future, you receive a fixed sum that is considerably larger than your purchase price. Let's use an example—a 10% municipal bond. That bond, if it matures in 1999, will cost you $394 per thousand, which means you pay $3,940 today to get $10,000 eight years from now. A $10,000 bond maturing in thirteen years will cost you $2,810. And, if you buy bonds the day your child is born, you can get a $10,000 bond maturing in eighteen years for only $1,730.

Zero coupons are not often called "zero coupons." Instead, investors should look for them under acronyms like STRIPS (Separate Trading of Registered Interest and Principal of Securities), TIGRS (Treasury Investment Growth Receipts), CATS (Certificates of Accrual on Treasury Securities), and M-CATS (with "M" standing for Municipal).

Many families like to use zero coupon bonds to save for college expenses because they can time the maturity dates to coincide with their students' tuition bills. Also, they know exactly how much money they will receive when those tuition bills come due.

There are, however, several drawbacks to zero coupon bonds, which families should be aware of before making this type of long-term monetary investment.

- Corporate bonds and municipal bonds may be called before they reach maturity, and if you miss the call, you may be in for a nasty surprise when you go to claim your money. Here's why. When a bond is called (usually because of declining interest rates) interest stops accumulating, and its value, therefore, freezes. The $10,000 face value you thought you were receiving could turn out to be little more than the bond's original cost (which may have been only a few thousand dollars). Treasury bonds are much safer, as they carry a no-call provision.
- Even though no income is distributed, tax must be paid yearly on the accrued interest. The exception is for zero-coupon municipals which are tax free (but somewhat rare).
- There is no way of knowing with any certainty what the value of the money will be when the bond matures. If interest rates rise, the value of the bond drops. If interest rates drop, the value of the bond rises. As a rule, corporate bonds have the highest yield, but also carry the highest risk.
- Investors take the risk that the issuer of their bond will be around 20 years from now to pay off the amount due. To be safe, avoid municipal bonds issued by small municipalities and corporate bonds with risky ratings (AAA is good, DDD is not). To be extra safe, buy mutual-fund corporate zeros or government backed Treasury zeros.
- Zero-coupons are relatively new investment tools, and the secondary market, should you want to get rid of your bond, is still a little thin. Zero-coupons cannot be traded as quickly as, say, a New York Stock Exchange listed security.

11. **Invest in Stripped Municipal Bonds.** Instead of selling bonds intact, with the principal due at maturity and interest payments along the way, some investment firms sell the two components separately. Investors have two options. They may buy the rights to the principal when the bond matures in X years, or they may buy one or more of the semi-annual coupon payments. In neither case do investors get interest payments. Instead, they buy at deep discount from the face value they will eventually receive. This makes them very similar to zero coupon municipal bonds, only without the disadvantages. Stripped municipals contain no call provisions nor are their earnings taxable (so long as the yield remains less than on the original bonds). As with zeros, families may plan ahead so the bond matures when their tuition payments are due.

12. **Invest in Life Insurance.** Insurance companies now offer Certificates of Annuity, which are very much like Certificates of Deposit (CDs), except the interest your money earns will be tax-deferred. Certificates come in one, three, and five year terms. The interest rate is guaranteed through to maturity. Sometimes you can withdraw up to 10% of your investment each year without penalty. And sometimes you can borrow up to 75% of the value of the contract. Two cautions: Ask about miscellaneous fees and administrative charges and be sure to buy only from highly rated companies (Look for A. M. Best reports in your library for ratings of the insurance industry).

13. **Innovation.** Keep your eyes open for new, innovative savings plans. Most large banks and insurance companies realize a lot of money can be made by "helping" families save for college, and are becoming increasingly innovative (and competitive) in their offerings. Weigh the plans carefully and look for hidden charges. Make certain you know the effective rate of return on your investment, not just the coupon rate or the interest rate. Here is one example of a recent stab at innovation:

The College Savings Bank in Princeton sells CDs based on the average cost (room, board tuition and fees) of 500 independent colleges. The interest rate of the CD is 1.5% lower than the average annual tuition increase at these colleges. In other words, if the index rises by 8.6%, the interest rate is 7.1%. Your upfront premium reduces the effective rate of your investment a percentage or so more, making the actual yield not that much higher than that offered by most passbook savings accounts. Participants in this plan also face steep penalties for early withdrawal; 10% of principal during the first three years, 5% thereafter. Plan originators realize investors could do better elsewhere, but like proponents of all prepaid tuition plans, what they are selling is security. Over time, families are assured that their CD will keep pace with college expenses, and that's not necessarily a bad way to invest. For more information CollegeSure CDs, call 1-800-888-2723.

IN WHOSE NAME—PARENT OR CHILD

The critical decision you must make, in any long-range capital accumulation plan, is whether the plan will be in your name, at your tax rate, or in the child's name, at the child's tax rate.

Obviously, the money will grow more quickly in the child's name because of the lower tax bracket. But when it comes time to pay tuition bills, the child's money is subject to a substantially heavier assessment. Colleges will demand 35% of the child's assets each year, but only 5.6% of parental assets.

Some financial advisors and planners fall all over themselves suggesting the tax advantages of accumulating money in the child's name. Let's see whether this is good advice. A family in the 35% bracket (this includes an allowance for state taxes) elects to make a yearly gift of $1,000 to a child, starting at birth. The money is invested at 8%. At the end of eighteen years, the kitty will be worth $34,892.

Had the family added $1,000 per year to a parental account, also invested at 8%, the money, under higher taxation, would have grown to only $28,662.

Now it's need analysis/family contribution time. For each of the next four years, the student's kitty is depleted by 35% of its value. The parental kitty, on the other hand, is depleted by only 5.6%. At the end of four years, the child's kitty has shrunk by $28,664 to $6,228. The parental kitty has shrunk by only $5,904 and is still a respectable $22,758.

So what should you do?

If there is no chance your family will qualify for aid, save in the child's name. Accumulate the money more quickly. And then spend it all on tuition.

If there is any chance for getting aid, save in the parent's name, make the smaller family contribution, and pad your college expenditures with need based aid.

Predicting aid eligibility is no easy task. Constantly changing tax laws and student assistance laws confuse professionals, to say nothing of those whose jobs do not depend on keeping up with Congressional activity. Here's what we advise. Assume the ratio between present earnings and assets and present college costs will hold for the future. Run your family through the Congressional Methodology in Appendix 1. Compare the estimated family contribution with the current costs of colleges of interest. If your family contribution is less than the cost of college today, you may qualify for aid in the future. Remember to divide the parental contribution component by the number you will have in college at least half-time (including parents) at any one time.

CONFUSED? STRANGLED BY LOOPHOLES AND RED TAPE?

If you're running into snags or all these techniques are confusing or require too much research, then request our free brochure We Can Help (Octameron, PO Box 2748, Alexandria, VA 22301). It describes our college admission and financial aid services. Neither cost very much and both can save you a bundle—both in money and in time.

Our Tuesday Special. We keep an experienced counselor on the phone every Tuesday from 10 AM until 4 PM EST, to answer questions you may have about college financing (or selection or admission). The conversation will cost you $30 which you may charge against your VISA or MASTER CARD. Call (703) 836-5480.

Part IV
The Major Money Sources

Chapter 9
The Colleges

RETHINKING YOUR IDEAS ABOUT ADMISSION

Unless you plan to attend one of the few remaining highly selective colleges, rid yourself of the thought that it's hard to get into college. It's easy. Over 80% of all students are accepted by the schools to which they apply.

In the old days, you applied to five or six schools; one or two where your odds were fifty-fifty, a couple where you had the edge, and a fall-back school that was sure to accept you. Today your selection strategy needs to be based on factors other than the possibility of rejection.

First and foremost you should consider the quality of education offered by each institution, but then you should consider the financial aid offerings. Look for:
1. Schools with innovative payment plans. These can ease the burden on the family budget.
2. Schools with innovative aid programs. These can channel money toward the "desirable" student.
3. Schools with mountains of cash. These can usually handle your "need."
4. Schools with a reputation for leadership in your selected field of study. They are likely to be well-endowed in your field.

Next you should remember that financial aid resources are limited. The first people in line are more likely to have their need met than the last.

Also, the intense competition for quality students translates into "no-need" awards and "preferential packaging."

Lastly, financial aid officers have some elbow room or leeway to re-assess family contributions, costs of attendance, and the contents of aid packages.

Given these words of wisdom, it's up to you to take action.
1. Apply "early decision" for both admission and financial aid—that way you should have all your need met.
2. Apply to colleges where your qualifications place you in the upper 25% of the applicant pool. That standing will have a significant impact on the composition of your aid package. Schools make no bones about that. In fact, a prestigious university went so far as to describe its preferential packaging policies in its catalogue."With a GPA of 3.6 and combined SATs of 1200 or more, your need will be met 80% by scholarships, 15% by loans and 5% by work. But with a GPA below 3.3 and SATs below 1050, the package will contain only 10% in scholarships, 65% in loans and 25% in work."
3. Always pair your applications. Don't apply to just one four-star school; apply to two. Don't apply to just one three-star school; apply to two. This may increase your number of non-reimbursable application fees, however, when you receive acceptances from schools of similar prestige, you may be able to play one against the other in an effort to improve the aid package. A school may not mind losing you to a lesser regarded college. But it will fight to keep you from going to a direct competitor.

IT DOESN'T HURT TO ASK

The financial aid sections of college catalogues are usually written in one of the murkier languages known to linguists. The structure emphasizes modifiers and contradictions—the writers' skill with the double negative surpassing even the most convoluted legalese. In their contents, pious generalities outnumber hard facts. And the overall tone can only be described as patronizing benefaction.

There are exceptions. Andrews University (MI) once called its aid philosophy the "stretch concept." You stretch and Andrews stretches. Or Messiah College (PA) provided an aid breakdown by program and by dollars, e.g., "Total aid this year from institutional grants, scholarships and tuition discounts is $896,171; from non-institutional private grants, $166,675; from federal and state government grants, $1,090,108; from loans, $2,127,510; and from work opportunity programs, $547,628." And Central College (IA) made no bones about using aid for recruiting. "Frankly, we're out to attract talented and academically-ambitious students and we'll reward them for their past performance as well as for their potential."

But such candor is seldom found. To get answers, you will have to write. Don't be bashful about writing. This is a buyer's market and you have the right to ask the colleges as many questions as they ask you. Your letter should raise questions about the availability of innovative payment and tuition aid plans of the type illustrated in the next two sections. And you should certainly obtain answers to the following questions:

1. Do you have a per-student-limit on the aid you provide? Reason: Some schools set ceilings, such as a $2,000 per student maximum.
2. Do I have to demonstrate a minimum amount of need to qualify for aid? Reason: Some schools will not consider students for aid unless they have at least $500-$800 need.
3. Do you have a standard "unmet need" figure for each aid recipient? Reason: Some schools will, automatically, leave each aid recipient $500 short. The formal name for this technique is "gapping." According to the NY Times, it is "the academic equivalent of short-suiting."
4. What is your expected "summer earnings" figure? Reason: It can range from $700 to $1,200. The colleges will expect that amount, whether it comes from the student's contribution or the parents' contribution (See Chapter 6).
5. Is there an application cut-off date for guaranteeing a student's unmet need? Reason: Some colleges say they can meet all need for students whose applications are received prior to Date X. But no such guarantee extends to students who apply after the cut-off.
6. Do you maintain financial aid "waiting lists" or accept students on an "admit-deny" basis? Reason: These practices mean financially needy students are welcome but they will not receive financial aid.
7. If I don't apply for aid in my freshman year, can I apply in subsequent years? Reason: You can't be prohibited from applying, however, you may get nothing because many colleges give priority to "continuing recipients."
8. How are "outside scholarships" packaged? Reason: Different colleges have different "aid philosophies." For example, one school in New York will take the first $300 of the outside scholarship and 20% of the rest and use it to replace a loan. What's left reduces the student's grant from that school. At other colleges, the outside scholarship merely replaces, on a dollar for dollar basis, collegiate grants, causing the poet Leider to ponder from her garret:

You found a nifty scholarship
To loosen the tuition grip.
But does this change what you must pay?
Or do they take your grant away?

Don't expect an outside scholarship to be applied to your family contribution. That seldom happens. But do search for a policy that at least permits it to replace part of the package's loan component.

9. What percentage of alumni contribute to the school's annual fundraising campaign? Reason: If you are worried about the college's financial survival, you can't ask for a corporate balance sheet. But you can check with the college's development office to learn whether the school has strong alumni support. In a recent year, at Randolph-Macon (VA), for instance, it was 62%. Other schools with high rates: Dartmouth (NH), 65.5%; Siena (NY), 65.1%; Williams (MA), 63.6%; and Centre (KY), 60.1%. When colleges have that kind of loyalty, they are not going to fold.

16 INNOVATIVE PAYMENT PLANS

1. **Installment Plans.** Realizing not many people can write a $2,000 or $4,000 check at the beginning of each semester, many colleges try to soften the blow by permitting you to spread the payments. Ask about installment plans. Here are the variants you may encounter.
   - Interest Policy: (1) No interest (2) Fixed interest (3) Interest on the remaining balance (4) No interest, but a one-time fee.
   - Down Payment Policy: (1) No down payment (2) Down payment of one-third or one-fourth.
   - Payment Frequency Policy: (1) Ten monthly installments (2) Two installments per semester (3) Four installments per semester.
   - A combination of these variants.
2. **Prepayment Discount.** Pay it all at once at beginning of the semester, and your tuition is discounted, sometimes by as much as 10-20%.
3. **Advance Payment Bonus.** Place some money into your account before it is due. The college will add a cash bonus each month to your credit balance. It can be a set dollar amount (e.g., $100) or it can be a percentage of the amount on deposit (e.g., 2-5%).
4. **Adjustable Rate Loans.** First we had the adjustable rate mortgages; now colleges are offering adjustable rate tuition loans. The University of Pennsylvania (PA), for instance, has become such a lender. One feature: The size of monthly payments will not vary. But because neither the total amount borrowed nor interest rates can be predicted—both tuition costs and interest rates fluctuate—plan participants will not know how long they must make their stable monthly payments. All they can be sure of is that the payments will continue long after graduations.
5. **Tuition Freezes.** A guarantee that tuition will hold for a set length of time or that it won't increase by more than a fixed percentage (e.g., 3%). A variant: Invoke tuition freezes in the service of retention and limit them to 3rd and 4th years of attendance.
6. **Guaranteed Tuition Plans I.** No Prepayment. Guarantees students their tuition will not be increased in their sophomore, junior, and senior years.
7. **Guaranteed Tuition Plans II.** Deposit Required. Same as preceding plan, but the college requires you to maintain a set sum on deposit—anywhere from $500 to $3,000. These plans may a have a financing option.
8. **Guaranteed Tuition Plans III.** Prepayment Required. Pay four years tuition in advance, at the rate which prevails in your freshman year. Parents who have the resources to make an out-of-pocket prepayment must decide whether the tuition increases they will be spared are worth more than what their money could earn in interest if it had not been used for prepayment. If the money is to be borrowed, parents usually have two choices: (1) In many cases, the sponsoring college will act as lender, offering the money at a favorable interest rate. Repayment, under such an arrangement, may extend from four to fifteen years. (2) Parents may consider raising the money by borrowing against the equity in their house. The interest rate may or may not be higher than the rate offered by the college. One advantage is that the equity loan will reduce the parents' asset position for need analysis. The resulting smaller family contribution could qualify their student for a student loan which will cover expenses not included in a tuition plan, such as room and board, books, travel, and miscellaneous. Another advantage is that interest payments on home equity loans of up to $100,000 are tax deductible.
9. **Guaranteed Tuition Plans IV. Other Types.** At some schools, the guaranteed tuition plan covers as many years as parents can pay in advance—one, two, three, or four. At others, the school will sweeten the pot by rebating say 10% of the payment at the end of each year.
10. **Guaranteed Tuition Plan V.** At some schools, families can purchase four year tuition packages in one lump sum. The amount you pay depends upon when the student will enter the university. For example, parents of a three-year old might pay $5600 to cover four years worth of tuition beginning in the year 2006. One catch: If the student is not admitted or decides to go elsewhere, some schools refund only the initial investment, and keep the

accumulated interest for themselves. Be sure to ask about this. The originator of this plan, Duquesne (PA) has since abandoned it because of lower-than-expected-returns in the bond market. The plan was financially too risky. Popularity is expected to diminish further as national plans and state plans get underway (see Chapters 8 and 11).

11. **Stretched Payments.** Not unlike a loan. Parents of students who do not qualify for aid defer a fixed amount of their tuition bill. They are given two years to pay the deferred amount and are charged a slight interest rate.
12. **Barter.** A usable service provided by you or your parents is exchanged for tuition.
13. **Three-Year Option.** The college offers a "time-shortened degree option" that permits students to satisfy graduation requirements in three years, saving one year in tuition costs.
14. **Choice of Accommodations and Meal Plans.** Do you need a spacious room with a spectacular view, or are you happy contemplating the backside of a dumpster? Do you need 21 meals a week in the college dining hall or would you rather cook for yourself when the daily special reads "Chef's Surprise or Mystery Meat?" Colleges are now giving you options. Some colleges have housing contracts that vary up to $2,000 per year, depending on location and type of room. Others offer several different meal plan plans. Cost difference: from $25 to $1,000 per year.
15. **Use of Credit Cards for Bill Payment.** Provides credit card holders with some flexibility but can cost them dearly in finance charges on unpaid monthly balances.
16. **Use of Electronic Bank Transfers.** A set amount is transferred from your account to the college treasury each month, without any human being ever touching the money.

37 INNOVATIVE STUDENT AID PROGRAMS

1. **Academic Scholarships.** Over 1200 colleges and universities offer scholarships—generally of the "no-need" type—to students who meet special excellence criteria in grade point averages, SAT/ACT scores, or class standing. See *The A's & B's of Academic Scholarships* (inside back cover)
2. **Low Interest Loans.** Many colleges have become low-interest lenders to offset Uncle Sam's yo-yo student aid policies and provide parents with certainty and stability in financial planning. At Lafayette (PA), for instance, parents who don't qualify for need-based aid can borrow $5,000 per year. Families have eight years to repay at 8%. At Fairleigh-Dickinson (NJ), families may borrow $15,000. They may take 10 years to repay at an interest rate equal to 9.5%. Lawrence (WI) loans have an interest rate that corresponds to the 91-Day Treasury Bill rate while the student is in school. Repayment of principal is deferred until after graduation. At that time, the interest rate floats to 4 points above the T-Bill rate. The Consortium on Financing Higher Education, a group representing thirty-two selective, expensive, primarily East Coast colleges has organized a loan program called SHARE. Parents of students at any of the consortium schools can borrow up to $20,000 per year and take up to 20 years to repay. Borrowers may choose between a monthly, variable rate loan (the prime rate plus 2%) or a one-year renewable rate (the prime rate plus 3-4%). Families may defer payment of principal for up to four years while the student is enrolled. Other costs include a guarantee fee of 5% of the loan amount. In some states, borrowers may secure a SHARE loan using a mortgage on their residential property. This requires a $50 application fee to Nellie Mae, and a $50-400 filing fee to their state, but then the interest paid on the loan may become deductible for Federal income tax purposes. For more information, call 1-800-634-9308.
3. **Quickie Loans.** Many colleges offer short term, small loans to tide students over in times of temporary financial crisis. These loans usually run from $100 to $500, but sometimes students can get up to $2,000.
4. **Replacing Loans.** Many schools will let you use outside scholarships to replace the loan component of your financial aid package. Some schools limit this bonus to bright students. Others will make the switch only if the student finds the scholarship before the loan processing begins. Students should also inquire if the school has a limit (e.g., $2000) to the total amount it will replace.

5. **Middle Income Assistance Programs.** Special scholarships and loans for middle-income families.
6. **Asset-Rich Families.** Land-rich families whose holdings disqualify them for assistance can get Gold Medal Scholarships at Jamestown College (ND).
7. **Family Plans.** Rebates or lower tuitions when more than one family member attends the college. And that includes not only brother and sister, but also Mom, Dad and Grandma. Examples: Trinity College (DC) gives a 33% discount to additional family members. At Santa Clara (CA), the first of three enrolled at the same time gets free tuition. Seton Hall (PA) will give the mothers of graduates a 50% tuition remission, while Pace University (NY) lets the parents of enrolled undergrads take courses free on a space available basis.
8. **Alumni Children.** Tuition breaks for alumni kids are also common. Colleges like to establish multi-generation relationships with families. That's how chairs get endowed and buildings get donated.
9. **Peace of Mind.** A few schools will waive tuition payments in part or in full for any enrolled student should the person primarily responsible for the student's support die or suffer total disability.
10. **Incentives for Academic Achievement.** Many colleges have special scholarships and awards for the top enrolled (continuing) students. At Wheaton (IL) this award is worth $1,000. At Bridgewater (VA) maintaining a 3.2 average nets a $500 tuition credit. And the University of Connecticut (CT) Credit Union will up student depositors' interest checks by 10% for each "A" received.
11. **Matching Scholarships.** Many schools will match church scholarships up to $500 or $1000. Other schools will match state regents awards.
12. **Remissions for Student Leaders.** Many colleges will provide free tuition to campus leaders, for example, officers of the student government, editors of the school publications. Again, this won't happen to you on admission. But you should know about it so that you can get a head start on your campaign for student body president.
13. **Remissions for Work.** At Warren Wilson (NC) and Blackburn (IL) students get free room and board. But they must put in fifteen hours of campus work every week. Berea (KY) charges no tuition to students of limited means, but requires them to work ten hours/week. Many other schools provide room and board for residence hall assistants and supervisors. You may not qualify in your first year, but it's an opportunity you should know about.
14. **Emphasis on Student Employment.** Many colleges have beefed up their placement offices to help students find on and off-campus employment. Here are some examples of especially noteworthy programs we've heard about over the past few years. Blufton College (OH) has budgeted over $300,000 for campus employment in a "Learn & Earn" program. Cabrini (PA) underwrites a "Job Squad." Princeton (NJ) assists students who want to become entrepreneurs. Cornell (NY), in a massive program, offers over 400 students $2,000 work grants in the hope of reducing their dependence on loans. Schools like Amherst (MA) use their formidable alumni network to locate student summer work opportunities. St. Edward's University (TX) entered into an agreement with a major retail chain for hundreds of part-time jobs. A special benefit of this program: It conserves federal work-study funds.
15. **Off-Hour Rates.** Many colleges set lower credit hour charges for courses taken during off hours—evenings and weekends. The difference can be as high as $300 per course.
16. **Recruiting Discount.** Bringing in another student can pay off. Some schools will reduce your tuition by as much as 10% for each of your recruits who enrolls.
17. **Moral Obligation Scholarships.** A new invention. Not a scholarship. Not a loan. The college provides money to the student and attaches a moral—but not legal—obligation to pay it back after graduation. A special sweetener: Until IRS changes its rules, the pay-back becomes a gift to the college and a tax deduction to the former student.
18. **Trial Attendance.** Some colleges say, "Try us you'll like us" and will offer new students a discount on their first few credits. For example, the school may offer free classes to high school juniors and seniors, it may let some students try the school for one semester for a low fee (e.g., $25), or it may run a free summer progam to give students a little taste.

19. **Bucking the Trend.** Some colleges seek to win the enrollment competition by freezing or even lowering tuition.
20. **Special Scholarship Drives.** Some schools have launched special fund-raising drives aimed at increasing their in-house financial aid kitty.
21. **Helping Students Find Scholarships.** Hundreds of schools have special offices to help students find grants, scholarships, etc.
22. **Older Student Remissions.** If you are over 25, Coe College (IA) will discount your tuition by 25%. If you are over 65, Lebanon Valley (PA), will discount your tuition by 50%. Many public schools offer free tuition to senior citizens as long as they are state residents and attending on a space available basis.
23. **Special Students.** Colleges look for students with unique interests or backgrounds. Many give special scholarships to any member of the National Honor Society or students who want to be math or science teachers. Grand Canyon (AZ) is looking for Eagle Scouts. Tarleton State (TX) offers rodeo scholarships. And, Arkansas College (AR) will pay you to play the bagpipes.
24. **Retention Awards.** Retaining enrolled students is important to colleges. Some offer financial inducements to get you back each year such as cancelling part of your loans.
25. **Travel Awards.** Some schools want to repay you either for a campus visit or, if you are enrolled, for the distances you must travel to obtain your learning. The Indiana Institute of Technology (IN) offers a $100 credit for a campus visit if you decide to enroll later on. Mobile College (AL) has a travel scholarship worth $500. Dartmouth (NH) and Stanford (CA) offer to pay the airfare of 80-100 of their brightest applicants, if they want to see the campus.
26. **Loan Origination Fee.** Stafford Student Loans carry a 5% loan origination fee. Some schools will pay your origination fee.
27. **Adopt-a-Student.** Some schools have convinced local churches and community groups to help students with scholarship money. In a variation of the adoption program, schools have asked corporations to extend grants and interest-free loans to students that will be forgiven if the student, after graduation, goes to work for the sponsor.
28. **Students Helping Students.** When that happens, it's a sign of good student morale and a friendly campus. Some examples we've heard about recently: At Azusa Pacific (CA), students raised $16,000 for scholarships in a phonathon. DePauw (IN) students did even better, raising $145,000. At Sarah Lawrence (NY), a scholarship auction netted $7,000. At Brown (RI), the University puts $4 in the college's scholarship fund for every hour student volunteers spend picking up litter on campus. At Georgetown (DC) students have organized a credit union and at Guilford (NC) students have raised over $100,000 to start a loan fund of their own. At Notre Dame (IN) students waived return of room-damage deposits, electing to contribute the money to a scholarship fund. Fitchburg State (MA) deposits all parking fines in a scholarship fund. And Davidson's (NC) senior class gift to the college was a $100,000 scholarship fund.
29. **Running Start.** High school students can spend their senior year, or the summer before their senior year on a campus, taking regular college work. St. Norbert (WI) and Mercer (GA) offer scholarships that will cover tuition but not room and board. Miami (OH) looks on such students as a farm club. Those who earn a 3.5 average are eligible for annual $1,000 scholarships if they enroll at the university following high school graduation. At Wesley (DE), any local student in the top 40% of the high school class (with combined SATs of at least 800) may take (and receive academic credit for) up to two courses each semester for free. Some questions to ask: Are the courses for college credit? If so, are the credits good only at the offering college or are they transferable?
30. **Help for the Unemployed.** Some schools offer free tuition to students from families whose major wage earner is unemployed.
31. **Free Tuition for Farmers.** Some schools offer up to a year of free tuition to farmers who have had to quit farming because of financial hardships.
32. **A Birthday Gift.** To celebrate its 100th anniversary, Dana (NE) let each of the school's 101 graduating seniors award a $4,000 scholarship to any new student who met Dana's

admission requirements. Goucher (MD) also celebrated its 100th birthday. It did so by allowing selected students to attend college for four years at 1885 tuition rates, $100/year. Note: Both of these opportunities are past, but keep your eyes open for similar "celebrations." Hood College (MD) has its centennial in 1993. According to its PR department, in 1992, some enrolled relatives of alumni (selected by a lottery) will be able to attend Hood for the same tuition paid by their relatives.

33. **Guaranteed Degree.** Some schools will allow graduates who are unhappy with their major (because they couldn't find a job, maybe) to return to the alma mater and major in another field, tuition-free, or at least at reduced tuition.
34. **Tuition Equalization.** To compete more effectively with public schools for top students, some private colleges offer their own tuition equalization programs. At Bard College (NY), first year students who were in the top ten of their high school class are charged only as much tuition as they would have paid had they gone to their state-supported school. The promise is good as long as they maintain a "B" average once in college.
35. **Automatic Scholarship.** Using income from its endowment, Illinois College (IL) offers an automatic $2,000 to each of the 800 students who enroll. Arkansas College (AR) offers an equally attractive gift to each entering freshman. If they remain in good standing through their senior year, during January term of their senior year, the school will pay transportation and housing expenses for two weeks of foreign travel. What fun!
36. **Toll-Free Numbers.** Hundreds of schools send financial aid recipients a toll-free number and the name of a "personal financial counselor" with whom to discuss financing options.
37. **Reward for Community Service.** The University of California, Berkeley (CA) will repay the federal loans of nearly 100 students who go into community service or public service when they graduate. Brown U. (RI) has a $500,000 kitty to repay the loans of graduates who teach or work for public service agencies. Xavier U. (OH) will give five full cost scholarships to students who spend 15 hours a week providing service leadership. The Washington Education Project lets college students earn academic credit for teaching nonreaders to read. Twelve schools currently participate, including New York University (NY) Boston College (MA) and Columbia College (IL).

For a more complete listing of what colleges offer which programs, get *College Check Mate* (see inside back cover).

IMPACT OF TAX REFORM

Now that we've looked at the variety of innovative payment plans and student aid programs offered by our nations colleges, you must understand how their benefits are lessened by two provisions in the tax bill:
1. **Interest on Consumer Debt is Not Deductible.** The deduction for interest paid on consumer debt (credit cards, auto loans, personal loans) has been phased out. This greatly diminishes the popularity of guaranteed tuition plans as the interest payments on the money most families must borrow to pay four years of tuition in advance will no longer be deductible (unless the family borrows against its home. Interest on mortgage payments is still deductible). The nondeductibility of consumer debt also impacts on the desirability of installment plans, low interest loan plans, and the use of credit cards for bill payments.
2. **Some Scholarships Will Be Taxed As Income.** The portion of a scholarship that exceeds tuition and fees is taxed as ordinary income. This means room and board scholarships may be taxed.

THE RICH SCHOOLS

Rich schools have more funds available for student aid than poor schools. They also have greater flexibility in making financial aid awards. It's their money, so they are better able to take individual circumstances into account than schools that dispense, in the main, public funds.

Wealth can be judged in one of two ways: (1) Total endowment or (2) endowment per enrolled student.

Here are schools with mountains of money:
Over $4 billion: Harvard.
Over $2 billion: University of Texas System, Princeton, Yale.
Over $1 billion: Stanford, Columbia, Texas A&M University System, Washington U. in St. Louis, MIT, U. of California.
Over $500 million: U. of Chicago, Rice, Emory, Northwestern, Cornell, U. of Pennsylvania, Dartmouth, Vanderbilt, Notre Dame, New York U., U. of Rochester, Johns Hopkins, Rockefeller U.
Over $250 million: CalTech, U. of Southern California, U. of Virginia, Duke, U. of Michigan, Brown, Case Western, Wellesley, Southern Methodist, U. of Delaware, Smith, Swarthmore, Grinnell, Carnegie-Mellon, Williams, Ohio State, Wake Forest U., Wesleyan, U. of Cincinnati, U. of Tulsa, Pomona, Trinity U., Amherst, George Washington U., U. of Richmond, U. of Pittsburgh, Berea, and Boston College.

Endowment per student leads to different rankings. Rockefeller U., $3,994,310; Princeton, $372,691; Harvard, $247,309; CalTech, $235,860; Rice, $218,396; Grinnell, $217,396; Swarthmore, $207,802; Yale, $196,960.

LEADERSHIP IN SELECTED FIELDS

Colleges that are acknowledged leaders in selected disciplines (e.g., the midwestern colleges in agriculture; the western schools in mining and geology) are usually heavily endowed by private sponsors in the areas of their special expertise. You are far more likely to find an agriculture scholarship at Iowa State than at Baruch College in New York City, or a petroleum engineering scholarship at the University of Oklahoma than at the University of the District of Columbia.

For opinions on who is best in what, ask the guidance office or school library to pick up a copy of **Rugg's Recommendations on the Colleges** ($14.95, Rugg's Recommendations, 5749 Colonial Oaks Blvd., Sarasota, FL 34232) or **The Gourman Report** (separate volumes for undergraduate and graduate programs, $14.95 each from Dearborn Trade, 800-245-BOOK. Another (perhaps better) way to get this kind of information is to speak with people you respect in your intended academic/career field. Find out where they went to school, and ask if they have any recommendations.

A tip: Very strong departments usually have scholarship funds they control themselves rather than the financial aid office. If you plan to major in a field in which a school is strong, consider dropping a note to the department head and ask about the possibility of departmental assistance.

DEALING WITH FINANCIAL AID OFFICERS

The median salary of financial aid directors, in 1990/91, was $38,256. You might want to keep that sum in mind as you get ready to explain how your $65,000 income has been ravaged by inflation to the point of making it impossible—absolutely impossible—to handle your family contribution. Remember that financial aid officers primarily dispense public funds—tax money—and such expenditures are usually quite controlled by law and regulations. Financial aid officers do have some flexibility in awarding the colleges' own funds and in treating changed circumstances—such unfortunate events as death, disability, disaster, and divorce. If you feel that any element of your award letter—the student's expense budget, your family contribution, or the mix of aid programs offered—should be changed, then go ahead and talk to the financial aid officer. But do so with sound reasons and, if necessary, with documentation. And keep in mind that one catches more Drosophila Melanogaster with honey than with vinegar.

Chapter 10
Uncle Sam

Every Student's Song

*Do Not forsake me, oh my Uncle
Before commencement day.
Do not change programs, oh my Uncle
Oh please, oh please—I say.
I do not know what costs await me,
I only know there will be more.
I need to have the grants you give me
Or be a drop-out, a lazy drop-out,
Or a starving sophomore.*

MEET YOUR UNCLE—UNCLE SAM

It's hard to meet college costs without also meeting Uncle Sam. For many students, applying for financial aid represents their first encounter with Uncle Sam.

One thing will become apparent very quickly. Getting things from Uncle Sam is no more pleasant an experience than giving him things, like your money at tax time. Here is what you should expect:

Uncle Sam likes forms. Lots of forms. Most of the forms have an awkward layout, an illogical sequence, and poorly written instructions for filling them out.

Uncle Sam makes a sharp distinction between "authorizations" and "appropriations." A program may be authorized, but that doesn't mean a nickel will be spent (appropriated) for it. Be careful when you hear about a much-heralded $10 billion student aid program. Before your expectations get too high, make sure the money for the program has actually been appropriated.

Uncle loves semantics and fine distinctions. His authorization bill may promise a chicken in every pot. But the enabling legislation, usually expressed in regulations, may define "chicken" as "any part of the bird," a claw, a feather... Or the definition may emphasize the avian nature of a chicken. The operative word then becomes "bird" and any bird can be substituted for a chicken—sparrow, pigeon, crow...

Uncle is a social engineer. After redefining chicken, he will turn his attention to the pot. He may rule that anybody who owns a pot large enough to hold a chicken is too rich to qualify for a fowl. Only owners of small pots can get birds—the smaller the pot, the bigger the bird will seem.

Uncle's promises don't hold for very long. Any program can be supplemented, altered, modified or rescinded in mid-year or near election time when it becomes important to hold down expenses and balance the budget.

Uncle likes to arm wrestle with himself. If the Administration doesn't like what Congress has mandated, it will delay, miss deadlines, base its case on budget figures that Congress had rejected (but not yet replaced), blow smoke over the issues, hold up regulations, or tie up appropriated funds.

Uncle's timing does not correspond to the academic cycle. When you want to start planning for the next academic year, usually in September, Uncle is not ready for you. By the time he can tell you what he will do for you, your plans are already made.

But when all is said and done, Uncle Sam is still your main source of financial aid. Warts or no warts, you had better learn to live with him and like him.

THE BIG SIX TODAY

Program	Level of Study Undergrad	Level of Study Grad	Need-Based Yes	Need-Based No	Part-Timers Yes	Part-Timers No	Need Analysis System
Pell Grant	X		X			X	Pell Grant
Stafford Loan	X	X	X			X	CM
PLUS	X			X		X	CM
SLS/Indep Undergrad	X			X		X	CM
SLS/Graduate Student		X		X		X	CM
SEOG	X		X		X		CM
CW-S	X	X	X		X		CM
Perkins Loans	X	X	X		X		CM

Most of Uncle's student aid flows through six gigantic programs. Three are student based—the Pell Grant Program, the Stafford Student Loan Program (formerly known as the Guaranteed Student Loan Program), and the PLUS/SLS Program (formerly known as ALAS—Auxiliary Loans to Assist Students). You apply for assistance under these programs and the money comes to you.

The other three programs—Supplemental Educational Opportunity Grants, College Work-Study and Carl D. Perkins Loans—are campus-based. That means, Uncle funds the programs, but gives the money to the colleges. The colleges, in turn, dispense the money to students in accordance with federal guidelines.

Program information is available by calling **The Federal Student Aid Information Center,** 800-4-FED-AID, Monday through Friday between 9:00AM and 5:30PM (Eastern Time). The hearing-impaired may call (301) 369-0518 (note: this second number is not toll free and collect calls will not be accepted). Trained staff is available to assist families in completing financial aid applications and correcting Student Aid Reports; to explain the Pell Grant Index, the Expected Family Contribution, and the purpose of the Student Aid Report; to answer questions about student eligibility; and to expedite loan payment problems. The number is NOT to be used for family financial counseling, to change information in your file, to make policy, or to expedite application processing. When you call, be prepared to spend a lengthy amount of time on hold.

If you want to find out if your application has been processed or if you want to request a duplicate SAR, you'll have to call (301) 722-9200.

If you suspect fraud, waste or abuse involving Federal student aid funds, please call the Education Department's Inspector General's Office at (800)MISUSED. You may remain anonymous, if you wish.

Uncle publishes a free booklet called **The Student Guide: Five Federal Financial Aid Programs.** Sometimes budget constraints cause it to be replaced with a 12-page fact sheet. In either case, you can request a copy (usually after the first of the year) by calling 800-4-FED-AID, or writing to The Federal Student Aid Information Center, PO Box 84, Washington DC, 20044.

STUDENT-BASED PROGRAMS

1. PELL GRANTS. These are Uncle's largest gift program. Over $5.5 billion in Pells will be dispensed to 3.4 million students in 1992/93. They are the foundation of student aid, the bottom layer of the financial aid package. But they can also be called Pinochio Grants. Why? Because for four consecutive years, Uncle did not hold to the award range which he promised. In one year, $1,800 became $1,750; in another $1,670; and in still a third $1,674. In 1987/88, the maximum grant was reduced from $2,100 to $1,400. How does this happen? Easy. Uncle doesn't request enough funds and then explains, unconvincingly, that more students applied to the program than he had expected. This excuse, combined with the 4.3% program reduction required by Gramm-Rudman caused the 1987/88 reduction to be the most dramatic of all. You may notice we didn't mention 1989/90 or 1990/91. In these most recent award years, a modern day miracle occurred. The entire maximum grant ($2,200 and $2,300 respectively) was actually funded.

So what will the award range be for 1992/93? Our prediction: The current range of $200 to $2,400 or 60% of the college's cost of attendance, whichever is less (although the Senate is pushing for a top award of $2,500). Both eligibility for an award and the size of the award are established under the need analysis system called the Pell Grant Methodology. If your family is judged capable of contributing more than $2,200 to college costs, as measured by that methodology, you probably won't qualify for a Pell Grant. If your family contribution is less, you should qualify. The smaller the contribution, the bigger the Pell Grant. A contribution of $2,200, incidentally, corresponds to a family of four, with an income of $35,000 and $42,000 in assets. It will show up as a "Pell Grant Index" (PGI) of 2200. *College Grants From Uncle Sam* (See inside back cover) has easy-to-follow worksheets for making your own eligibility calculation.

Let's pinpoint the dual concept of an award range $200 to $2,400—or 60% of costs, whichever is less. Say you are eligible for a maximum grant and you will attend a college costing $3,000. Your award? $1,800—because 60% of $3,000 is $1,800 which is less than the maximum grant of $2,400. Now suppose you go to a school which costs $6,000. Your award: $2,400—because $2,400 is less than $3,600 (60% of $6,000).

Application for a Pell Grant can be made on every need analysis form in use, right after January 1 of the year in which you will attend college.

Important: Apply for a Pell Grant, even when you know you are not eligible. Colleges and the states expect you to do so and won't consider you eligible for other awards unless you have been turned down for a Pell Grant.

You will receive your "Student Aid Report" on the same form as your "need-analysis report." In other words, when you receive a copy of your expected family contribution from the kind folks doing your need analysis, you will find your Pell Grant Index alongside it.

If you are eligible for a Pell Grant, your Student Aid Report (SAR) will have three parts: (1) The Information Summary; (2) The Information Review Form; and (3) The Payment Voucher. If you are not eligible, it will have just the first two. Follow the SAR's directions carefully. Check the information on which your eligibility/lack of eligibility was determined. It's in Part 2 of the form. If the processor made an error, use Part 2 to let the processor know immediately.

If no corrections are to be made, sign the SAR and send a photocopy of both sides of Part I to the financial aid office of each institution to which you are applying. Move quickly on this so schools can make Pell Grant eligibility part of your financial aid package. When you decide which school to attend, send all three parts to that school's financial aid office. It will use the Pell Grant Index to determine the actual amount your award. Remember to send the SAR even if you are to receive no award. The financial aid office may need it to determine eligibility for state or campus based programs.

Things to Know About Pell Grants:
- If you are a half-time or three-quarter-time student, you receive 50% or 75% of your award respectively.
- Thirty percent of all applications must be validated by the college financial aid office. That's when you have to produce copies of income tax forms and other documents for a comparison check. Other applications are selected for validation by the federal government. These returns are selected for validation on the basis of "pre-established criteria." That's bureaucratese for "something smells fishy."
- If there is a drastic change in personal or financial circumstances after you have applied, let the financial aid officer know at the schools to which you have applied. He or she will explain how to use the Correction Application to file for a "special condition" calculation This generally means you can use expected (1992) income to have your eligibility recalculated.

2. STAFFORD STUDENT LOANS.
Formerly called Guaranteed Student Loans, the program has been renamed in honor of retired Senator Robert T. Stafford (R-VT).

Eligibility. Everyone, no matter what their family income, is required to demonstrate need to qualify for a Stafford Loan. They will also have to apply for a Pell Grant and attend school at least half-time.

Loan Limits. Freshmen and sophomores may borrow up to $2,625 per year. Juniors, seniors and fifth year undergraduates may borrow up to $4,000 per year. The maximum undergraduate loan amount is $17,250. Graduate students may borrow up to $7,500 per year to a maximum of $54,750 (less any money they borrowed as an undergraduate).

Loan Origination Fee and Insurance Fees. Lenders will subtract 5% loan origination and, generally, a 0-3% insurance fee. Shop around. At this writing, PHEAA (in Pennsylvania) charged no insurance fee.

Interest Rate. For new borrowers after July 1, 1988: 8% increasing to 10% in the fifth year of repayment. Loans taken out prior to that carry a 7%, 8% or 9% rate (depending on the specific year of the loan) and remain at 7%, 8% or 9%, even if they are renewed.

Interest Subsidy. Uncle Sam pays interest on the loan while you are a student and for a six-month grace period after you complete your studies.

Minimum Annual Repayment. $600.

Years to Repay. 5 to 10.

Who Makes Loans? Private lenders—Banks, S&Ls, Credit Unions, Insurance Companies. Also some states are in the lending business.

Application Procedure. Obtain loan application from lender. Fill out application. Send application to college for certification by financial aid officer. After that, application is processed through lender and guaranteeing agency before loan is dispensed. Many lenders advertise overnight processing, however, we advise you to allow two months for the paperwork flow.

Under certain circumstances, loans can be deferred, postponed, canceled or considered for forbearance.

For more information on all aspects of Staffords, see *College Loans From Uncle Sam* (See inside back cover).

3. PLUS/SLS LOANS

Program is not based on financial need. These loans may be used to replace some or all of your expected family contribution.

Two Types of Loans:

(1) Parents Loans to Undergraduate Students (PLUS). Parents may borrow $4,000 per year per undergraduate, dependent student to maximum of $20,000. This amount does not include money borrowed in the Stafford Loan program.

(2) Supplemental Loan to Students (SLS). Independent, undergraduate students and graduate students may also borrow up to $4,000 per year to a maximum of $20,000. This amount does not include money borrowed in the Stafford Loan program. Note: You must apply for both a Pell and a Stafford before you may be considered eligible for an SLS. Also, in an attempt to curb rising defaults, Congress may prohibit first year students from receiving SLS loans or find some other way to keep that handful of unscrupulous "for profit" schools from abusing the federal loan/grant system.

Insurance Fees. PLUS/SLS loans carry no origination fees, but lenders may charge up to a 3% insurance fee.

Interest Rate. 3.25% above the bond equivalent of the 52-week T-bill. The rate is adjusted annually (based on the last auction prior to 1 June), but is not to exceed 12%. The current rate is an all time low 9.34%.

Repayment. To begin within 60 days of taking out the loan. Extends from 5 to 10 years. Repayment can often be deferred while the student is in school, however, interest keeps accumulating.

Caution. The combined total of a PLUS/SLS Loan and other aid cannot exceed the student's cost of attendance.

Who Makes Loans? Private lenders—Banks, S&Ls, Credit Unions, and some states.
Application procedures are similar to Stafford Loans. Under certain conditions, loans can be deferred, postponed or canceled.
For complete information on PLUS/SLS Loans, see *College Loans From Uncle Sam*.

COLLEGE-BASED PROGRAMS

4. SUPPLEMENTAL EDUCATIONAL OPPORTUNITY GRANTS. SEOGs are administered by colleges with funds received from Uncle Sam. $520 million per year.
Size of awards. From $100 to $4,000 per year for each year of undergraduate study.
Criteria for Selection. Need and availability of funds. Be smart. Apply early. Priority goes to those students receiving Pell Grants.
Part-Timers. 10% of funds may be set aside, at the school's discretion, for support of less than half-time students.

5. COLLEGE WORK-STUDY. CW-S is administered by colleges with funds received from the federal government. About $600 million per year.
Eligibility. Undergraduate and graduate students.
Criteria for Selection. Need and availability of funds. Be smart. Apply early.
Program Description. On-and-off campus employment. Salary must be at least as high as minimum wage (currently $4.25 per hour). You cannot earn more money than your award stipulates. Thus, if you receive a $1,000 CW-S award, your employment lasts until you earn $1,000 and then it is terminated for that academic year. Employment may not involve any political or religious activity nor may students be used to replace regular employees.
Part-Timers. 10% of funds may be set aside, at the school's discretion, for support of less than half-time students.

6. PERKINS LOANS. The college acts as lender, using funds provided by the federal government. Approximately $156 million in new lending capital; almost $1 billion in "revolving fund" capital (money paid back by borrowers).
Eligibility. Undergraduate and graduate students.
Part-Timers. 10% of funds may be set aside, at the school's discretion, for support of less than half-time students.
Criteria for Selection. Need and availability of funds. Be smart. Apply early.
Size of loan:
(1) $4,500 total in first two years of college.
(2) $9,000 between third year status and graduation (minus what you borrowed in first two years).
(3) $18,000 for graduate study (minus what you borrowed as an undergraduate).
Minimum Annual Repayment. $360
Interest rate. 5%.
Interest Subsidy. No interest while a student or during 9-month grace period following graduation.
Repayment. 10 years.
Under certain circumstances, loans can be deferred, postponed or canceled.
For more information on all aspects of Perkins Loans, please see *College Loans From Uncle Sam*.

On Defaulting

Uncle Sam rewards and punishes colleges for their ability or lack thereof to collect on outstanding loans. Schools with small default rates (under 10%) will get an increased infusion of loan capital; schools with high default rates (25% or more) may soon get zilch. If you're interested in access to this attractive program, check school default rates during the college selection phase (by means of a letter to the college).

Uncle Sam can also punish you if you are one of the defaulters. He can notify credit bureaus which will damage your credit rating. Or, he can withhold your income tax refunds until your loan is paid off (last year alone, the IRS collected $261 million!). As the default problem gets worse (at some schools, in some programs, it is as high as 85%), Uncle Sam is getting tougher, as he should. In our book, defaulters are eclipsed by even the most parasitic protozoa!

LOAN CONSOLIDATION

Students with federal loans (Stafford, Perkins, SLS, and HPSL) in excess of $5,000 who don't land a high paying job when they graduate, may want to look into loan consolidation. Under "consolidation" you can stretch repayment over a greater number of years—as many as twenty-five. That means your monthly payments will be 6% smaller for loans of $7,500, 16% smaller for loans of $10,000 and 31% smaller for loans of $45,000. It also means the total of all your repayments will be greater than if you had opted for the regular repayment route. Consolidation also lets you opt for graduated repayments. Under this choice, the monthly payments start small and increase over time—supposedly at the same rate as your earning power. For more information on consolidation, check with the institution that gave you your loan or your state guaranteeing office (addresses in *College Loans from Uncle Sam*). If neither offer consolidation, contact SALLIE MAE, 1050 Thomas Jefferson Blvd. NW, Washington DC, 20007 or NELLIE MAE, Loan Consolidation Department, 50 Braintree Hill Park, Suite 300, Braintree, MA 02184.

NOTE: Other education related debt, including PLUS loans and HEAL loans, cannot be consolidated; however, the amount of your HEAL loans may be considered in determining the length of the consolidation repayment period (the greater the debt, the greater the time you have to repay).

THE BIG SIX TOMORROW

Federal student aid is here to stay, but with reauthorization of the higher education acts underway (deadline: September 30, 1992), who knows what student aid will be like in the future. The only certainty is that money is tight and until the deficit is under control, Uncle Sam will not be getting any more generous with education dollars. **Not-So-Fun Fact:** According to the Congressional Budget Office, 14.3% of every tax dollar goes to pay the interest on our $277 billion national debt (only defense and social security get more); a measely 2.2% of every tax dollar goes to education and training.

Here are some of the ideas under consideration:

Increase financial support from the business community. President Bush wants money for education to come from somewhere other than Washington, and business is the natural alternative. After all, it has the most to benefit from an educated workforce.

Change in the Congressional Methodology. Some of the proposals include: reducing the expected contribution from student income from 70% to 45%; excluding from assets the value of a home, farm, or small business for families earning less than $40,000 per year; easing the definition of "independent student," and tightening the defintion of "independent student."

Tighten loan policies. Uncle Sam loses a lot of money as a result of student loan defaulters. In addition to tightening default regulations, for several years, the Administration has been trying to get a new type of loan program going. Income Contingent Loans (a concept Milton Friedman first experimented with in the 1970s) are still a $10 million pilot project—Congress steadfastly refuses to give the Administration the $50 million it wants. Loan limits are $4000 in each of a student's first two years, $5,000 thereafter to a maximum of 50,000. Repayment begins 90 days after the recipient ceases to be at least a half-time student and may continue for up to thirty years. At no time may repayment exceed 15% of income (that's where the income contingent part comes in). The interest rate is 3% above the t-bill. There are no federal subsidies, even while the student is in school (i.e., the interest accumulates, even though the student doesn't have to pay anything).

Increase the size of Pell Grants. The Administration has proposed raising Pells to $3,700/year, but restricting eligibility to eliminate middle income families from the program. Congress has proposed indexing Pells to guarantee they keep up with inflation.

Increase borrowing limits. To help middle income families made ineligible for Pells, the Administration would raise Stafford Loan limits to $3,500 per year for students in their first two years of college and $5,000 for years 3, 4, and 5. Similarly, SLS loans would rise to $6,000 per year for undergrads and $10,000 per year for graduate students.

Simplify student aid applications and create a single need analysis formula. The current form has an intimidating 150 data elements for students to complete. Furthermore, families must frequently file more than one application if they want to be considered for all types of assistance.

Eliminate new contributions to the Perkins Loan. Schools could still use the nearly $1 billion in the revolving fund, but Uncle would make no new contributions.

Eliminate State Student Incentive Grants. The Administration threatens this every year.

Begin a National Information Campaign to promote the importance of higher education and the availability of federal student aid. Research shows that early counseling is the most effective way to increase going-to-college rates.

Limit federal aid to students attending programs lasting at least 600 hours. This would get rid of program abuse on the part of many for-profit trade schools.

Introduce optional graduated repayment schedules for students with Stafford and SLS loans. This would ease the payment burden for recent graduates, who presumably will earn more as the promotions roll in.

National College Savings Bank. Many variations have been put before Congress. Most involve allowing families to set up accounts much like an IRA. The contributions, as well as the interest that accrues would not be taxed until the child finishes his or her undergraduate education.

Focus on volunteerism. A national service plan will be drafted, but whether or not it will have ties to student aid is still in question. Here are the two plans recently considered by the House and Senate:

1. The National Service Act, introduced by Representative Augustus Hawkins (D-CA). This bill would provide $25 million in grants to colleges and universities for them to use to create or expand community services activities for students; for example, the Student Literacy Corps or Student Tutorial Corps. In exchange for participating in these activities, students would be eligible for Stafford Loan deferment and Perkins Loan cancellation. Hawkins' bill also authorizes the creation of an American Conservation Corps (for urban revitalization) and a Youth Service Corps (to encourage elementary and secondary students to perform community service).

2. The National and Community Service Act, introduced by Senator Edward Kennedy (D-MA) and Senator Orrin Hatch (R-UT). This bill creates full- and part-time volunteer opportunities for people to earn vouchers for school or for buying a home. It also allows students who participate the chance to reduce their Perkins and Stafford Loan debts by up to 70%, depending on the length of their volunteer service.

Neither of these plans would replace current student aid programs.

Chapter 11
The States

All states maintain extensive programs of grants, scholarships, tuition assistance, fee reductions and loans. Last year, 1.4 million students received $1.7 billion in need-based state aid and 252,301 shared in $217.5 million of non-need-based aid.

States making the most awards: New York, Pennsylvania, Illinois, Ohio, California, Minnesota, New Jersey—in that order.

States spending the most (over $50 million each) on student aid: New York, Illinois, California, Pennsylvania, Texas, New Jersey, Ohio, Michigan, Minnesota, Massachusetts, Florida, and North Carolina—in that order.

States where the average award is $1,000 plus—Alaska, California, Connecticut, District of Columbia (we know it isn't a state), Florida, Illinois, Indiana, Iowa, Kansas, Massachusetts, Michigan, Minnesota, Missouri, Nevada, New Jersey, New York, North Carolina, Pennsylvania, Rhode Island, and Texas.

How do middle income families fare in the competition for state funds? Last year, students from families with incomes over $20,000 represented 38% of all grantees, receiving 37% of the funds dispensed. Not bad!

A SUMMARY OF STATE PROGRAMS

The following summary table describes current state student assistance programs other than state participation in the Stafford Student Loan and PLUS/SLS Loan programs. With regard to these two programs, every state has a guaranteeing agency, either its own or a non-profit organization operating within the state's borders, that administers the loans. **College Loans From Uncle Sam** gives the addresses and phone numbers of these special agencies.

Here is an explanation of the table's columns.

Need-Based Programs. These are grant programs awarded on the basis of financial need. Both are generally restricted to undergraduate study.

Column 1—In-State Study. Self-explanatory.

Column 2—Some Other States. This indicates your state has signed a reciprocity agreement with one or more states.

Column 3—Merit Programs. Generally, there are three kinds of merit programs. The first type is based on financial need; however, there is an academic threshold you must attain (such as a B average) to be eligible. The second program is based on academic accomplishment. But you must demonstrate financial need to qualify for a monetary award; otherwise, your recognition will be honorary. The last type of program is based solely on academic accomplishment. Your award is not affected by your financial situation. Funding for merit-based programs is increasing more than twice as fast as funding for need-based programs (17% vs. 7%), as states don't want to lose their best students to other states.

Column 4—Special Loans. These are loans separate from the loans authorized under the Stafford and PLUS programs. In Alaska, it's an extremely generous program that requires two years of residency for eligibility. Undergraduates may borrow $5,500 per year at 8%. In Minnesota, SELF loans enable students to borrow $4,000 per year at 1.5% above the 91 day T-bill rate. In Maine, residents may borrow up to $20,000 per year at an interest rate 1% below the prime. In Virginia, residents may borrow up to $15,000 per year at 1.5% above the prime rate. For all these plans, the loan money is usually secured through tax-exempt bonds issued by the state or an authorized non-profit agency operating in the state. In some cases, out-of-state students attending a school in the state underwriting the loans may benefit from the low interest rates.

Column 5—Teaching. To increase the supply of teachers, many states have instituted special loan programs for students willing to become teachers, with "forgiveness" features if the students actually end up in classrooms. If the students don't go into teaching, they must repay the aid. Some programs limit their benefits to students who teach in a shortage area. This could mean a subject area like math or science. It could also mean a geographic area like rural America or the inner-city. The states listed here are those with programs in addition to the federally funded (state administered) Paul Douglas Teacher Scholarships program.

Column 6—Special Fields. This category covers a variety of programs designed to increase representation in other fields in which the state believes it has shortages. These fields may include medicine, nursing, special education, bilingual education, etc. Many graduate programs are included in this category.

Column 7—Minority Group Programs. Usually, the beneficiaries of these programs are Blacks, Hispanics, and Native Americans (Eskimos, Indians, and Aleutians).

Column 8—Work-Study. State operated programs similar to the federal work-study program.

Column 9—Veterans. Special state benefits to state residents who served in the Armed Forces, usually during periods of hostilities.

Column 10—National Guard. State educational benefits for serving in the state's National Guard. These are in addition to federal benefits.

Columns 11, 12, 13. Special benefits to state residents who are dependents of deceased or disabled veterans, or POWs, MIAs, or police/firefighters killed on duty.

Column 14—Military Dependents. These states let military personnel and their dependents stationed within the state's borders, attend in-state universities at lower in-state tuition rates.

Column 15—Tuition Savings Plans. To encourage early planning for college costs, many states allow families to purchase "Baccalaureate Bonds," the income from which is tax exempt if used to pay college expenses. These bonds are generally available through banks and brokerage houses. A second type of savings plan is the "Prepaid Tuition Plan" in which parents have the chance to guarantee four years of tuition at any of the state's public (or in some instances private) colleges by making either a lump sum investment or periodic payments. The amount depends on the child's date of entry into college and the degree of flexibility parents desire in withdrawing funds. The state invests the money and pays the student's tuition when he or she enters college, and takes the risk of actually guaranteeing tuition. While sophisticated investors can probably achieve a higher rate of return than in either of these plans, the fact is, most families are not comfortable playing investment games. They want an easy way to guarantee they'll have saved enough money for their children's education, and these plans do work!

State or Territory	1. In-State Study	2. Some Other States	3. Merit Programs	4. Special Loans	5. Teaching	6. Special Fields	7. Minority Gp Programs	8. Work-Study	9. Veterans	10. National Guard	11. Deceased or Disabled Veteran	12. POW or MIA	13. Police/Fireman Killed on Duty	14. Active Duty	15. Tuition Savings Plan
Alabama	X		X		X	X				X	X	X	X		X
Alaska	X	X	X	X	X	X	X			X		X		X	X[1]
Arizona	X		X		X		X			X				X	
Arkansas	X		X		X	X					X	X	X		X
California	X		X		X	X	X	X	X		X	X	X	X	
Colorado	X		X	X		X	X	X	X	X		X	X	X	X
Connecticut	X	X	X	X	X	X	X	X	X	X	X	X		X	X[1]
Delaware	X	X	X	X	X	X				X	X	X	X		
DC	X	X		X											

State or Territory	1. In-State Study	2. Some Other States	3. Merit Programs	4. Special Loans	5. Teaching	6. Special Fields	7. Minority Gp Programs	8. Work-Study	9. Veterans	10. National Guard	11. Dependent of Deceased or Disabled Veteran	12. Dependent of POW or MIA	13. Dependent of Police/Fireman Killed on Duty	14. Active Duty	15. Tuition Savings Plan
Florida	X		X		X	X	X	X			X	X		X	X
Georgia	X		X		X	X				X			X	X	
Guam	X		X	X	X	X								X	
Hawaii	X		X	X					X					X	
Idaho	X		X		X			X	X	X	X	X		X	
Illinois	X		X						X	X	X	X	X		X
Indiana	X		X		X	X	X	X		X	X	X	X		
Iowa	X		X			X	X	X		X					X
Kansas	X		X			X		X		X	X	X		X	
Kentucky	X		X		X	X		X		X	X		X	X	X
Louisiana	X		X		X	X			X			X		X	
Maine	X	X	X	X	X	X	X			X	X		X	X	
Maryland	X	X	X	X	X	X	X			X	X	X	X		X[1]
Massachusetts	X	X		X	X			X	X	X	X	X	X		
Michigan	X		X	X			X	X	X	X	X				X
Minnesota	X	X	X	X		X	X	X	X	X	X	X		X	
Mississippi	X				X	X				X	X	X	X	X	
Missouri	X		X		X								X	X	X[1]
Montana	X		X				X	X	X		X	X		X	
Nebraska	X														
Nevada	X		X	X	X	X	X	X	X	X	X	X	X		
New Hampshire	X	X	X	X		X					X	X		X	X
New Jersey	X		X		X		X		X			X	X	X	X[1]
New Mexico	X	X	X			X	X	X	X	X	X		X	X	
New York	X		X	X	X	X	X		X		X	X	X		X[1]
North Carolina	X		X	X	X	X	X		X	X	X	X	X		X
North Dakota	X	X	X			X	X			X	X	X	X	X	
Ohio	X	X	X							X	X	X	X	X	
Oklahoma	X		X		X	X	X					X			X
Oregon	X		X		X	X	X			X			X	X	X
Pennsylvania	X	X	X	X	X			X	X			X		X	X[1]
Puerto Rico	X									X					
Rhode Island	X	X	X			X		X							X
South Carolina	X		X	X	X	X	X			X	X	X	X	X	
South Dakota	X		X		X				X	X	X	X			
Tennessee	X		X		X	X	X			X	X	X	X		X
Texas	X		X	X	X	X	X	X	X	X	X	X	X	X	X
Utah	X		X		X	X				X	X			X	
Vermont	X	X		X	X	X		X							
Virgin Island	X	X	X			X				X					
Virginia	X		X			X	X	X		X	X	X		X	X
Washington	X	X	X		X	X		X						X	X
West Virginia	X	X	X	X	X	X				X	X		X	X	X
Wisconsin	X	X				X	X		X	X	X			X	X
Wyoming	X		X		X					X	X	X	X	X	X

[1]Legislation has been introduced or is under review.

INNOVATIVE STATE PROGRAMS

No two states have the same programs. Here are some you should ask about. Your questions might lead you to little-known or special opportunities.

Reciprocal Arrangements I. Besides the major reciprocal arrangements between states, lesser arrangementts often permit students living near the state's border to study in the adjoining state at in-state tuition rates. For example, students living in Minnesota may take classes in Wisconsin, South Dakota, North Dakota, and Iowa.

Reciprocal Arrangements II. Authority to study out of state when desired course program is not offered in state. Such arrangements are often supervised by consortia such as WICHE (PO Drawer P Boulder, CO 80301) which covers Alaska, Arizona, Colorado, Hawaii, Idaho, Montana, Nevada, New Mexico, North Dakota, Oregon, South Dakota, Utah, Washington and Wyoming; the Southern Regional Education Board (592 10th Street, NW, Atlanta, GA 30318) which operates in the Academic Common Market for undergraduate or graduate studies in the southern states; and the New England Regional Student Program administered by the New England Board of Education (45 Temple Place, Boston, MA 02111).

Reciprocal Arrangements III. WICHE has introduced an even larger reciprocal study program in which students may pay reduced tuition at any of the 55 state schools in the region. The reduced rate equals resident tuition plus 50%; a large savings over regular non-resident rates.

Tuition Equalization. These programs reduce the difference in tuition costs between in state public and private colleges. Examples: Alabama, Florida, Georgia, Iowa, Kentucky, North Carolina, Ohio, Texas, Virginia and West Virginia. Last year, these states made grants worth over $87.5 million.

Grant Programs I. Most states provide special assistance to students attending private colleges in state. Such awards are need based.

Grant Programs II. Some states provide need-based assistance to residents attending schools out-of-state. Examples: Alaska, Connecticut, Delaware, District of Columbia, Maine, Maryland, Massachusetts, New Hampshire, Ohio, Pennsylvania, Rhode Island, Vermont, West Virginia, and Wisconsin. These states made 26,539 grants last year, worth $20.16 million.

Paul Douglas Teacher Scholarship Program. Uncle Sam will fund 10,000 awards for high school graduates with an interest in teaching. Each state establishes its own selection criteria and selects recipients. The awards range up to $5,000 per year, but may not exceed financial need. Students must teach two years for every year the award is received (one year for those who teach in a shortage area). Otherwise the students must repay the money.

Robert C. Byrd Honors Scholarship Program. Uncle Sam also funds an $8 million honors scholarship program. Again, each state establishes its own criteria and selects recipients (at least 10 scholars per Congressional District). The awards are $1,500 for one year of academic study. They are not based on need and may be used at any school (except foreign schools).

National Science Scholars Program. Uncle Sam's newest state administered program will award renewable $5,000 scholarships to HS seniors who have demonstrated outstanding academic achievement in the physical, life or computer sciences, mathematics, or engineering. Scholars are nominated by their home state; the final selection belongs to the President (in consultation with the National Science Foundation). Two awards per Congressional District.

Innovative programs. Be on the lookout for these. There is a lot of action on the state level—some of which will result in important new programs (by the same token, some of these plans will be allowed to fizzle). Current state plans:

- **New York:** Liberty Scholarships. New York guarantees to pay the non-tuition costs of low income families who attend school in New York.
- **Michigan:** Tuition Incentive Program (TIP). Low income students can get free tuition at community colleges. Those who complete community college are eligible for a $2,000 voucher for use at any of Michigan's four year colleges.
- **Illinois:** College Savings Bonds. Illinois was the first state to encourage families to save for college expenses via tax-exempt (non-callable) zero coupon bonds. In Illinois, you receive an additional grant (up to $420) if you use the bonds to pay for college expenses.
- **Florida and Alabama:** Both have state-wide computer networks that provide students with (free) individualized lists of potential sources of financial aid. It can be found in high

schools, vo-tech centers, colleges, universities, prisons, and vocational rehab centers.
- **Arkansas:** Academic Challenge Scholarships provide the lesser of $1000 or tuition to any student who completes designated college prep courses in HS, has a minimum ACT score and meets financial need requirements. Louisiana, Texas, Florida, New Mexico, Indiana, Maryland and Oklahoma are enacting similar plans, thanks to the hard work of Patrick Taylor, a Louisiana oil man who has been pioneering the concept that many young people drop out of HS because they perceive it as a dead end. Promise them a college education if they can meet the admission standards, and you'll see a drastic increase in levels of educational achievement.
- **Virginia and Texas:** Special incentive grants to induce student of one racial group to attend a state public college or university in which another racial group makes up a significant proportion of the student body.
- **Colorado, Florida and Minnesota:** Colorado's Postsecondary Options Plan, Florida's Dual Enrollment Plan and Minnesota's Postsecondary Enrollment Options Act allow public HS students to take courses at no charge at any college in the state that will admit them (the Florida program is restricted to state schools). Students receive both high school and college credit for their work.
- **South Carolina and New Mexico:** South Carolina waives tuition for residents aged 60+ who attend state schools. New Mexico allows students age 65+ to take courses at public colleges for $5 per credit hour (on a space available basis).
- **Oregon:** Visto. This new program will allow students age 16-19 to earn vouchers of $25 for every 8 hours of volunteer work. Vouchers may be used for payment of tuition and fees.
- **Kansas:** Youth Education Service (YES) Program in which Kansans would receive financial rewards for their good work; an average of $1,000 each. The money goes to students who serve as classroom assistants or tutors for disadvantaged students in elementary, junior, or senior high school.

Directory of State Agencies

Alabama
205-269-2700
Student Assistance Program
Alabama Commission on Higher Education
One Court Square, Suite 221
Montgomery, AL 36197

Alaska
907-465-2962
Alaska Commission on Postsecondary Education
Box FP, 400 Willoughby
Juneau, AK 99811

Arizona
602-255-3109
Commission for Postsecondary Education
3300 N. Central Avenue, #1407
Phoenix, AZ 85012

Arkansas
501-324-9300
Department of Higher Education
114 E. Capitol
Little Rock, AR 72201

California
916-322-5043
Student Aid Commission
PO Box 510845
Sacramento, CA 94245-0845

Colorado
303-866-2723
Colorado Commission on Higher Education
1300 Broadway, 2nd Floor
Denver, CO 80203

Connecticut
203-566-2618
Department of High Education
61 Woodland Street
Hartford, CT 06105

Delaware
302-577-3240
Delaware Postsecondary Education Commission
State Office Building
820 N. French Street
Wilmington, DE 19801

District of Columbia
202-727-3685
DC Office of Postsecondary Education Research and Assistance
1331 H Street NW, #600
Washington, DC 20002

Florida
904-487-0049
Office of Student Financial Assistance
Department of Education
1344 Florida Education Center
Tallahassee, FL 32399

Georgia
404-493-5446
Georgia Student Finance Authority
2082 East Exchange Place, #200
Tucker, GA 30084

Hawaii
808-948-8213
Hawaii State Postsecondary Education Commission
Bachman Hall, Room 209
244 Dole Street
Honolulu, HI 96822

Idaho
208-334-2270
State Board of Education
650 West State Street, Boise, ID 83720

Illinois
708-948-8550
State Scholarship Commission
Client Support Services
106 Wilmot Road
Deerfield, IL 60015

Indiana
317-232-2350
State Student Assistance Commission
964 N. Pennsylvania Street
Indianapolis, IN 46204

Iowa
515-281-3501
Iowa College Aid Commission
201 Jewett Building
9th and Grand
Des Moines, IA 50309

Kansas
913-296-3517
Board of Regents, State of Kansas
Suite 609, Capitol Tower
400 West 8th Street
Topeka, KS 66603

Kentucky
502-564-7990
Higher Education Assistance Authority
1050 US 127 South, Suite 102
West Frankfort Office Complex
Frankfort, KY 40601

Louisiana
504-922-1011
LA Student Financial
  Assistance Commission
PO Box 91202
Baton Rouge, LA 70821-9202

Maine
207-289-2183
Finance Authority of Maine
Maine Education Assistance Division
State House Station, #119
One Weston Court
Augusta, ME 04330

Maryland
301-333-6420
State Scholarship Board
2100 Guilford Avenue, Room 207
Baltimore, MD 21218

Massachusetts
617-727-9420
Board of Regents of Higher Education
Scholarship Office
330 Stuart Street
Boston, MA 02116

Michigan
517-373-3394
Michigan Higher Education
  Assistance Authority
PO Box 30008
Lansing, MI 48909

Minnesota
612-296-3974
Minnesota Higher Education
  Coordinating Board
Capitol Square Building, #400
550 Cedar Street
St. Paul, MN 55101

Mississippi
601-982-6570
Board of Trustees of State
  Institutions of Higher Learning
Student Financial Aid
3825 Ridgewood Road
Jackson, MS 39211-6453

Missouri
314-751-3940
Coordinating Board for Higher Education
PO Box 1438
Jefferson City, MO 65102

Montana
406-444-6594
Commission of Higher Education
35 South Last Chance Gulch
Helena, MT 59620

Nebraska
Contact Individual Schools Directly

Nevada
702-784-4666
Financial Aid Office
U. of Nevada, Reno, Room 200 TSSC
Reno, NV 89557

New Hampshire
603-271-2555
New Hampshire Postsecondary
  Education Commission
2 Industrial Park Drive
Concord, NH 03301-8512

New Jersey
609-588-3272, 800-792-8670
Department of Higher Education
Office of Student Assistance
4 Quakerbridge Plaza, CN 540
Trenton, NJ 08625

New Mexico
505-827-8300
Commission on Higher Education
1068 Cerrillos Road
Santa Fe, NM 87503

New York
518-474-5642
Higher Education Services
  Commission
99 Washington Avenue
Albany, NY 12255

North Carolina
919-549-8614
State Education Assistance Authority
Box 2688
Chapel Hill, NC 27515

North Dakota
701-224-4114
Student Financial Assistance Program
Capitol Building, 10th Floor
Bismark, ND 58505

Ohio
614-466-7420
Ohio Board of Regents
30 East Broad Street, 36th Floor
Columbus, OH 43266-0417

Oklahoma
405-521-2444
Oklahoma State Regents for
  Higher Education
500 Education Building
State Capitol Complex
Oklahoma City, OK 73105

Oregon
503-346-4166
State Scholarship Commission
1445 Willamette Street, #9
Eugene, OR 97401

Pennsylvania
717-257-2800, (PA) 800-692-7435
Higher Education Assistance Agency
Town House, 660 Boas Street
Harrisburg, PA 17102

Rhode Island
401-277-2050
Higher Education Assistance Authority
560 Jefferson Boulevard
Warwick, RI 02886

South Carolina
803-734-1200
South Carolina Tuition Grants Agency
PO Box 12159, 411 Keenan Building
Columbia, SC 29211

South Dakota
605-773-3134
Office of the Secretary
Department of Education and
  Cultural Affairs
700 Governors Drive
Pierre, SD 57501-2291

Tennessee
615-741-1346, TN 800-342-1663
TN Student Assistance Corporation
404 James Robertson Parkway
Parkway Towers, Suite 1950
Nashville, TN 37243-0820

Texas
512-483-6340
Higher Education Coordinating Board
Box 12788, Capitol Station
Austin, TX 78711

Utah
801-538-5247
Utah State Board of Regents
335 W.N. Temple, 3 Triad, Suite 550
Salt Lake City, UT 84180-1205

Vermont
802-655-9602
Vermont Student Assistance Corp.
Champlain Mill, Box 2000
Winooski, VT 05404

Virginia
804-225-2141
Council of Higher Education
James Monroe Building
101 North 14th Street
Richmond, VA 23219

Washington
206-753-3571
Higher Education Coordinating Board
917 Lake Ridge Way, GV-11
Olympia, WA 98504

West Virginia
304-347-1211
Higher Education Grant Program
PO Box 4007
Charleston, WV 25364

Wisconsin
608-266-2578
State of Wisconsin Higher
  Educational Aids Board
PO Box 7885
Madison, WI 53707

Wyoming
307-766-2116
University of Wyoming
Student Financial Aids
Box 3335, University Station
Laramie, WY 82071

Guam
617-734-2921, x3657
Financial Aid Office
University of Guam
Mangilao, Guam 96923

Puerto Rico
809-758-3350
Council on Higher Education
Box 23305, UPR Station
Rio Piedras, PR 00931

Virgin Islands
809-774-4546
Board of Education
Commandant Gade, OV #11
St. Thomas, VI 00801

Part V
The Big Alternatives

Ok. You are willing to pick up a little maturity along with your education. You are willing to invest some extra time into earning a baccalaureate. And you want to start your professional career without the staggering burden of student debt. What can you do? You can investigate two major alternative methods of financing an education: (1) Letting the boss pay for it or (2) letting the militay pay for it.

Part V covers a wide variety of employee tuition plans—from those found in Madison Avenue corporate offices to those sponsored by the US Military. You can pick up nearly $3 billion along these routes.

Chapter 12
Letting the Boss Pay for It

COMPANY TUITION AID

Until 1984, you could go to work for a company that had a tuition reimbursement plan (and about 20 million employees were covered by such plans), take college courses on your own time, and let the employer foot the bill.

The Deficit Reduction Act of 1984 changed all this. It ruled that courses had to be job-related to qualify as a benefit. Courses not job-related, but paid for by the employer, had to be declared as taxable income.

That ruling pulled the rug out from what had promised to become a major alternative program for young people. The reason: Jobs at the bottom are usually so narrowly defined that few of the many educational explorations required for a degree could pass the "job-related test." Why would a shipping clerk need a course in American History?

While hurting people at the entry level, the law has little impact on the educational pursuits of the higher-ups. A manager might justify a course in English Literature to improve her writing skills and a sales manager could qualify for an Anthropology program to better understand the cultural factors that influence buying.

The Tax-Reform Act of 1986 brought back the exclusion of non job-related tuition benefits, but limited the exclusion to $5,250. Since then, Congress has continued to extend the exclusion, but on a year-to-year basis. The exclusion expires every September 30, however, as 1 in 10 workers currently make use of this benefit, we anticipate another extension.

Beginning in 1991, graduate students, as well as undergrads, became eligible for this exclusion!

Reimbursements for courses that are job-related remain 100% tax excludable for both undergraduate and graduate students (with no dollar ceiling).

Even if your employer does reimburse you for tuition, and the reimbursement remains a tax-free benefit, there may be some strings attached. For example, you may have to stay with the firm for a set number of years after you graduate, or maintain a certain grade point average while in school. These requirements are only fair—after all, employers help employees with their education for the good of the company, not just for the good of the employee. Ford is one company that realizes this; it pays 100% of any course approved by a boss.

Still, a better program for the beginner is Cooperative Education.

COOPERATIVE EDUCATION

Cooperative Education is a program which combines formal studies with an off-campus job related to your major. The money earned on the job will, in most cases, cover college costs. In some schools, practically the entire student body participates in cooperative education. Examples: Northeastern University (MA), College of Insurance (NY), GMI Engineering & Management Institute (MI). There are three common methods for rotating between school and work:

- **The alternating method.** Under this method, you are a full-time student for a term or semester, with the cycle repeating itself until you graduate—usually in five years.
- **The parallel method.** Here you attend classes part time and work between 15 and 25 hours a week. You may be a student in the morning and a worker in the afternoon, or vice versa. This method, too, may require five years for degree completion.
- **Extended day method.** The student works full-time and attends school in the evening.

Employers like the co-op program, considering it, in the Wall Street Journal's words, "a source of realistic, work-oriented, future full-time employees."

Some statistics about cooperative education: 900 participating colleges, 50,000 participating employers, 200,000 enrolled students who earn $1.3 billion each year. The biggest employer, offering the widest choice of work sites, academic plans and career fields: Uncle Sam (over 7,000 students).

More information on cooperative education:

1. Two booklets—one for undergraduate and one for graduate cooperative education programs—free—National Commission for Cooperative Education, 360 Huntington Avenue, Boston, MA 02115.
2. Linking up with Uncle Sam's cooperative education program—the directory *Earn and Learn* with descriptions of 16,300 federal coop positions, the 36 sponsoring agencies, the career fields and location of work sites, and the names of the 750 participating colleges (see inside back cover).

JUNIOR FELLOWSHIPS

This is another program from Uncle Sam; 5,000 openings for students in the upper 10% of their class with financial need. Junior Fellowships provide opportunities to work in a federal agency during all academic calendar breaks—winter, spring, summer. There is no restriction on college choice. Students can put together as much as $12,500 in earnings over four years. Often, a professional position with Uncle is available following graduation.

The program is poorly advertised. In consequence, it has never been filled to authorized levels. Last year, for example, the program had 3,600 vacancies. Application and selection are made in the senior year in high school.

For more information on Junior Fellowships, get *Earn and Learn,* as described above.

INTERNSHIPS

It's hard to draw the line between cooperative education and internships. Two general distinctions: The alternating involvement between formal studies and work, in cooperative education, extends throughout a student's college career, while internships often last only one semester or one summer break. Participants in cooperative education always get a paycheck; interns may or may not. In fact, the more "desirable" the internship, the less the pay. Those that do pay generally offer students from $75 to $100 per week.

More information on internships:

National Society for Internships and Experiential Education, 122 St. Mary's St., Raleigh, NC 27605.

Chapter 13
Putting on the Uniform

Don't overlook the military as a source of financial aid. You can pick up tuition dollars before you enter the service, while in uniform, and after being discharged.

There are programs for active duty personnel and programs for being in the Reserves or the National Guard. And there are programs for officers and programs for enlisted people.

Military tuition benefits are dispensed with no reference to financial need. You qualify for them, whether you are rich or poor. But they are not free. The military will want something in return. As a minimum it will require you to get a haircut, salute superior officers and give a few years of your time.

Service Status	Typical Programs
Before Entering Service	Military Academies ROTC Medical Programs One-Shot Programs
In Service	Off-Duty Programs Commissioned Officers Formal Programs Leading to Associate, Baccalaureate, Graduate Degrees
After Service	Montgomery GI Bill Veterans Educational Assistance Program (VEAP) Dependent Benefits

BEFORE ENTERING SERVICE

Military Academies

The academies are extremely competitive. Good grades, extracurricular activities, leadership and athletic excellence are in demand. So are superb health and solid SAT scores. On the math portion you should have 600+ and your combined score should be 1200 or more. Contact the academies during your junior year of high school. Most appointments are made by Representatives and Senators. Tell your elected officials about your interest. Make sure they open a file on you in their offices Keep feeding that file with your achievements. Also add recommendations. Make sure you obtain recommendations from people who are deemed important by the elected officials.

ROTC Scholarships

The military has 2-year, 3-year, 4-year and even 5-year ROTC scholarships. These scholarships will pay for tuition, books and fees. You will also get a $100 monthly allowance. Note: The Army now limits its ROTC awards to 80% of tuition, or $7,500, whichever is greater. Some schools offer free room and board to ROTC scholarship winners, but room, board, transportation and miscellaneous expenses are generally your responsibility. A 1200 SAT with 600+ on the math portion will enhance your chances for an ROTC scholarship. So will a varsity letter and membership in the National Honor Society. Application here, too, should be made during your junior year of high school. There will be an interview. Before the interview, brush up on current affairs. Also, be prepared to give your reasons for seeking a military career. An interest in a science or engineering major will enhance your chances of winning an ROTC scholarship. ROTC is not offered at all colleges. The services will provide you with a list. You have to select a college from that list and secure admission yourself.

The Regular ROTC Program

This is not a scholarship program. Students join the program in their freshman year, at colleges that offer ROTC. For two years they march and salute for free. In their junior and senior years, participants do get paid: $100 per month.

ROTC-Coop Education Combination

The Army reserves cooperative education positions for some ROTC cadets in nearby Army installations. These positions, which provide added earnings, will also lead to federal employment after the participant has served on active duty.

Military Medical Programs

See Chapter 20

One-Shot Programs

On occasion, the Navy and the Air Force need highly specialized technical people and will use financial aid as a recruiting tool. For instance, the Air Force has a "College Senior Engineer Program" for students in electrical, nuclear, astronautical and aeronautical engineering. Students can sign up during their junior year. In their senior year, they will receive $1740 or $900 per month. After graduation, they are called to active duty, attend Officer Training School and serve as a commissioned officer.

MORE INFORMATION

Academies:

Admissions Office, USMA
606 Thayer Road
West Point, NY 10996

Director of Cadet Admissions
USAF Academy
Colorado Springs, CO 80840

Candidate Guidance
US Naval Academy
Leahy Hall
Annapolis, MD 21402

Admissions
US Merchant Marine Academy
Kings Point, NY 11024

Admissions
US Coast Guard Academy
15 Mohegan Avenue
New London, CT 06320

ROTC:

Army ROTC
Ft. Monroe, VA 23651
800-USA-ROTC

Hqs. US Marine Corps
Code MRON-6
Washington, DC 20380
800-843-8762

Navy Opportunities Info Center
PO Box 9406
Gaithersburg, MD 20898
800-327-NAVY

AF ROTC
Recruiting Division, Building 500
Maxwell AFB, AL 36112
800-423-USAF

IN SERVICE EDUCATIONAL BENEFITS

Commissioned Officer

Each year, the services select hundreds of officers to attend graduate schools. The chosen officers receive full pay and allowances and have all their educational expenses met while pursuing their master's degree or doctorate.

Off-Duty Programs

All services have arrangements with civilian colleges and not only permit but encourage off-duty course work, with the services paying up to 90% of the tuition costs (amount varies with rank and length of service). Through credit transfers and arrangements with accrediting institutions, such off-duty courses can be accumulated to gain credit for associate, baccalaureate or even master's degrees.

Concurrent Bonuses and Benefits

Through the National Guard and Army Reserves, you can receive approximately $5,000 in education benefits under the Montgomery GI Bill. You can also earn cash bonuses—for example $1,500-$2,000 for enlistment in the reserves; up to $2,000 for completing advanced training in the National Guard. The Army Reserve, National Guard, and the Regular Army also offer repayment on federal student loans as an incentive for enlistment in selected skills. In the Army Reserve, repayment is 15% of the outstanding loan or $500, whichever is greater, (to a maximum of $10,000), for each year of service. In the National Guard, repayment is 15% of the outstanding loan or $1,500, whichever is greater, for each year of service. And, in the Regular Army, repayment is 33% of the loan or $1,500, whichever is greater (to a maximum of $10,000), for each year of active service.

AFTER SERVICE

The Montgomery GI Bill

Congress enacted a new GI Bill which affects everyone enlisting after July 1, 1985. It is a contributory system. The soldier or sailor or airman, while on active duty, allocates $1200 to an educational fund. The Veteran's Administration will then add up to $9600 ($7800 for a two year enlistment). By the end of the enlistment, the participant has $10,800 for tuition money. The Army sweetens the pot with education bonuses for enlisting in what they call critical "Military Occupation Specialties" (MOS) such as the infantry. This could add up to $14,400 (for a four year enlistment) to the $10,800 already earned. The Army calls this bonus "The New Army College Incentive." Call 1-800-USA-ARMY for more information. The Navy is planning to start its own matching fund—look for details on the "Navy Sea College Fund" to be released soon.

The Veteran's Educational Assistance Program

For those of you who enlisted before July 1, 1985, don't worry. The military has education benefits for you, too. In fact, you will find the military educational incentives to be similar. VEAP is also a contributory system. The participant can pledge up to $2700, either in monthly installments or as a lump sum. The government will match the contribution 2 for 1, up to $5400. At the end of your enlistment you have as much as $8100 for tuition money. As additional incentive, the Army College Fund will add up to $18,300 (for a four year enlistment) if you sign up for a critical MOS. If you are eligible for these benefits, take advantage of them soon. VEAP is likely to be phased out sometime in the near future.

Dependents Education Assistance

Wives and children of veterans who died or were totally disabled as the result of service qualify for Veterans Administration educational benefits. These benefits are also extended to dependents of former Prisoners of War and soldiers classified as MIA—Missing in Action.

State Educational Benefits

Most states have aid programs for Veterans and their dependents. See Chapter 11 and write to your state's Office of Veteran Affairs (addresses in *Need A Lift*, PO Box 1050, Indianapolis, IN 46206, $2.00).

BENEFITS FOR MILITARY DEPENDENTS

Army

1. Army Emergency Relief. Loans and scholarships for spouses and unmarried children of active, retired or deceased Army members. For scholarships, apply by March 1 to Army Emergency Relief, 200 Stovall Street, Alexandria, VA 22332.
2. Summary of Educational Benefits. Request DA Pamphlet 352-2, Headquarters, Department of the Army DAAG-EDD, Washington, D. C. 20314.

Air Force

Air Force Aid Society. Grant program ($1,000) for children of active, reserve, retired or deceased Air Force members. Loans for children and spouse of active, reserve, retired or deceased Air Force members. Also loans for active, reserve, or retired AF Members themselves. Same terms as the federal Stafford Loan program (Chapter 10). Air Force Aid Society, Education Assistance Department, 1745 Jefferson Davis Highway, Suite 202, Arlington, VA 22202-3410.

Navy/Marines

Dependent's Scholarship Program for U.S. Navy, Marine Corps, and Coast Guard Dependents. More than 75 Navy-oriented organizations currently sponsor scholarships or offer aid for study beyond the high school level. Dependent sons and daughters of Navy, Marine Corps, Coast Guard, and former members are eligible for these scholarships or aid. Information and current application forms may be obtained by writing the Commander, Naval Military Personnel Command, NMPC-602, Navy Department, Washington, D. C. 20370-5000. Applicant should state whether or not he/she is a qualified dependent. 1-800-255-8950.

ASSOCIATION BENEFITS FOR THE FAMILIES OF FORMER MILITARY

Former military families tend to congregate in organizations after leaving the service. Nearly every military association sponsors student aid programs to the children of its members. The table that follows is a sample. For a comprehensive list, obtain the useful annual book *Need a Lift?* published by he American Legion, PO Box 1050, Indianapolis, IN 46206. Cost: $2.00, prepaid.

AMVETS Memorial Scholarship

$1,000/year scholarships for 4 years. Veteran, H.S. senior (son or daughter of veteran), U.S. citizen. Forms available after January 1. AMVETS National Headquarters, attn. Scholarships, 4647 Forbes Blvd., Lanham, MD 20706-9961.

Reserve Officer Association

Henry J. Reilly Memorial Scholarships. 100 awards for undergraduate and graduate studies. Opens Feb. 1. Closes April 30. Scholarship Fund, ROA, 1 Constitution Avenue, N.E., Washington, D. C. 20002.

Retired Officers Scholarship Program

Not a grant, but an interest-free loan program. Maximum: $7,500 ($1,500/yr.) spread over five years, for unmarried dependent children of active and retired commissioned members of the military. Coast Guard, NOAA and Public Health Service. Apply to Administrator, Scholarship Committee, TROA, 201 N. Washington St., Alexandria, VA 22314.

SCAMP

Scholarships for Children of American Military Personnel (SCAMP) Awards for children of armed service personnel who served in Vietnam and were killed in action, missing in action, or prisoners of war. $2,500/$3,500. SCAMP Grants, 136 S. Fuller Ave., Los Angeles, CA 90036.

COORS

Coors has a $500,000 scholarship fund for children of American veterans. Write: Coors Veteran's Memorial Scholarship Fund, PO Box 370, McLean VA 22101, by 15 March.

A POSSIBLE STRATEGY

Go on active duty for three or four years. While on active duty, take off-duty courses (for which the military will pay up to 90% of the tuition costs) and make sure the courses add up to an associate degree. At the same time participate in the Montgomery GI Bill. When you are ready for discharge, you will have credit for two years of college and a tuition kitty of at least $9000 (more if you were in the infantry) to help you pay for the last two years of college. By the time you get your degree, you will be one, or at the most, two years older than your contemporaries who did not go into service. That minor disadvantage will be offset by somewhat greater maturity and self-confidence. And you'll probably be free of debt.

Part VI
Special Opportunities

Chapter 14
Private Sources with Few Strings

COCA COLA SCHOLARS FOUNDATION, INC.

150 scholarships per year, 50 for $5,000/year, renewable for up to 4 years at the college of one's choice. 100 are $1,000 per year, renewable for up to 4 years. Applicants must be high school seniors. Applications available only through senior's high school guidance office. First application must be postmarked on or before October 31. Course of study in any discipline. Merit-based scholarship emphasizing leadership. Write to Coca-Cola Scholars Foundation, 3060 Peachtree Road, NW, Suite 1000, Atlanta, GA 30305.

ELKS NATIONAL FOUNDATION

Nearly 2000 awards, over $2.5 million awarded. HS senior, US citizen. Scholarship, leadership. Application from officer of local Elk Lodge. By February 1.

HATTIE M. STRONG FOUNDATION

Interest-free loans for college students within one year of graduation. Up to $2,500/year. Repayment based on monthly earnings. Hattie M. Strong Foundation, 1735 Eye St., NW, Suite 705, Washington, DC 20006.

HITACHI FOUNDATION

The Yoshiyama Award. Given annually to 6-8 high school seniors. Not a scholarship and not based on academic achievements. Students may not nominate themselves. Award is accompanied by a gift of $5,000 over two years with no restrictions as to how gift is to be used. Award is in recognition of outstanding community service by high school students. Nominees need not be college-bound. No later than May 15. Nominations to Yoshiyama Award, PO Box 19247, Washington, DC 20036. (202) 457-0588.

KNIGHTS TEMPLAR EDUCATIONAL FOUNDATION

Loans. Has helped over 70,000 students. $3,000 per year to $6,000 maximum. Last two years of college (or grad school). 5% interest. Apply through divisions. Division address from Grand Recorder Secretary, Knights Templar Educational Foundation, 14 E. Jackson Blvd., Suite 1700, Chicago, IL 60604.

PICKETT & HATCHER EDUCATIONAL FUND

Low interest loan program. Residents of Southeastern United States, US Citizen. Preference in areas other than law, medicine, or ministry. Has helped 18,000 students. Scholastic ability, character, financial need. Request application blanks in Oct. from Pickett & Hatcher Educational Fund, P.O. Box 8169, Columbus, GA 31908. May 15 deadline.

Chapter 15
Money in Your Community

Just about every community offers scholarship assistance to its young citizens. The grants can vary in size from one hundred dollars to several thousand.
Community awards are circumscribed in their geographic coverage. They may include:

Single state. Examples: the *MESA* program in California; *The New Hampshire Charitable Fund/Student Aid Program*; the *Piper Scholars* program in Texas.

A county. Example: *The Blandin Foundation's* awards in Itasca County, Hill City and Remer school districts.

Your city. Examples: (1) New York City has established a *City Volunteer Corps* (CVC) for 17-20 year old New York City residents. In addition to receiving a weekly stipend, these community service volunteers are presented with a $5000 college or vocational scholarship upon completion of one year of full-time service. For more information on this program, please write CVC Volunteer Corps, 838 Broadway, New York, NY 10003. (2) Students attending public school in Cleveland (grades 7-12) accumulate scholarship money for good grades; $40 for each A, $20 for each B, and $10 for each C. In 1989 nearly 20,000 students received money. Similar (smaller) programs have now been started in Wellington, OH and Englewood, NJ.

Your community. Look for scholarship bulletins from civic associations, businesses, PTA chapters, social and professional clubs, fraternal organizations, patriotic and veterans organizations. Some communities do very well by their students. For example, the journalist Carl Rowan has founded a program called "Project Excellence" that awards over $250,000 per year to graduating seniors in the Washington DC area. In addition to private donors in your community, you should look toward larger local foundations. There are nearly 400 community funds nationwide, with assets totaling more than $6 billion. From this money, these foundations award nearly $100 million to education projects annually!

Your high school. Many high schools have established information clearing houses to work in conjunction with the guidance office. Students (and their parents) may attend workshops on college financing; they receive individual assistance on filing aid applications; they have access to current financial aid literature; and in some instances, they can tap into computerized scholarship data bases. ALL FOR FREE! Some schools have even created foundations to provide "last dollar scholarships" for students with exceptional financial need. Example: The Scholarship Fund of Alexandria (VA).

I Have A Dream Ten years ago, the very wealthy Eugene Lang promised college scholarships (and extra counseling/tutoring) to an entire sixth grade class at his former elementary school in East Harlem. In 1986, he created the I Have A Dream Foundation to assist other people in starting similar projects. He has became a hero. Today, about 10,000 students benefit from over 140 "I Have A Dream" projects in 41 cities across the country. Unfortunately, needy students can't apply directly for this assistance; they can only hope someone will adopt their class (and at a minimum investment of $300,000/class, benefactors are hard to find). It's still too early to tell whether the program has been effective, but corporate America is jumping on the bandwagon...witness "The Pepsi Challenge" in which the soft-drink company provides up to $2,000 in college scholarship money for "at-risk" students at selected high schools in Detroit and Dallas who meet certain GPA and attendance requirements.

Dollars for Scholars. Dollars for Scholars chapters are community-wide, volunteer-operated scholarship foundations affiliated with the *Citizen's Scholarship Foundation of America,*

Inc. (CFSA) A local board of trustees organizes and publicizes its program in the community, then goes on to raise local funds for distribution to local students. CFSA provides non-profit status, guides, and materials for chapter operations, and access to CFSA-sponsored scholarships and related programs. All funds raised locally are distributed by a local awards committee. Chapters pay a one-time affiliation fee of $50. An annual $25 fee maintains a chapter's certification. For further information, or for a complete, "How to Organize" kit, write: Volunteer Services Coordinator, PO Box 297, St. Peter, MN 56082, or call 1-800-248-8080 or (507) 931-1682.

There is no central registry for these kinds of opportunities. You must learn about them yourself. Read the local newspaper carefully, especially the page devoted to club and community affairs. Visit the Chamber of Commerce. It might keep track of business and corporate scholarships offered in your area. Also visit the American Legion Post. The legionnaires take a special interest in helping people with their education.

Chapter 16
Are Your Parents Eligible?

You may be eligible for financial assistance because your parents were in the military service or presently work for a particular company or belong to a union. A trade group or association can become a source of aid; so can parental membership in patriotic, civic or fraternal associations.

Locating these opportunities will require a systematic approach and considerable parental cooperation. The matrix below can help organize your search strategy

Eligibility Category	Where to Start Looking
Military Service	*Need A Lift?* $2.00 from The American Legion, Attn: Emblem Sales, PO Box 1050, Indianapolis, IN 46206. Also Chapter 13.
Employment	Personnel Director
Union	Secretary of Local or *AFL-CIO Guide to Union Sponsored Scholarships and Awards.* $3.00. AFL-CIO Publications Office, 815 16th St., N. W., Rm. 209, Washington, DC 20006.
Trade Group/Trade Associations	Gale's *Encyclopedia of Associations*
Patriotic/Civil/Fraternal Associations	Gale's *Encyclopedia of Associations*

Here are some samples of the kind of information you will uncover. Remember, these are only a few of the many opportunities.

WHERE DO YOUR PARENTS WORK?
Scholarships
Many companies sponsor scholarships for employee children as part of their fringe benefit programs.

- **Merit scholarships.** Approximately 1500 renewable, need-based awards (ranging from $500 to $4,000) sponsored by over 400 corporations for employee children who are Merit Program Finalists (see *The A's & B's of Academic Scholarships*).
- **General scholarships** for employee children. Examples: Westinghouse Family Scholarships, Whirlpool, GEICO, Food Fair and State Farm.
- **FEEA Fund Scholarships** for federal employees and members of their families. 200 awards ranging from $500 to $1,500. By May 1. The Federal Employee Education and Assistance Fund Scholarship Award, 8441 W. Bowles Ave., Suite 200, Littleton, CO 80123.

Loans

A growing number of large concerns help make it easier for employee children to participate in the Stafford Student Loan program (see Chapter 10). The companies put up a reserve against loan defaults, then hire firms like United Student Aid Funds to administer the program and find banks to act as lenders. Ford, General Electric, Gillette, Texaco, Time, Winn-Dixie are among the 150 that provide this service. To find out if your company has such a plan, call United Student Aid Funds toll-free (800) LOAN-USA.

Federal government employees and members of their families should request information on FEEA educational loans and scholarships from FEEA, Washington, DC FEEA is a sponsor of TERI loans, a plan in which credit worthy families may borrow from $2,000-$20,000/year. The interest rate floats at 1.5% above prime. FEEA offers Stafford Loans (GSLs), PLUS loans and SLS loans. FEEA, 8441 W. Bowles Ave., Suite 200, Littleton, CO 80123.

ARE YOUR PARENTS MEMBERS OF

A Trade Group or Association?

Owners and employees of member firms may be eligible. Examples: *National Continental Association of Resolute Employers; National Office Products Association; National Association of Tobacco Distributors.* Look up addresses in Gale's *Encyclopedia of Associations*

A Patriotic/Civic/Fraternal Association?

Among many organizations making awards to members and members' children: *Knights of Columbus; Beta Sigma Phi; 100F/Rebekah; International Order of Job's Daughters; United Daughters of the Confederacy* (61 Awards); Yes—even the *Society for the Preservation of Barber Shop Quartets* has sixteen scholarships. Look up addresses in Gale's *Encyclopedia of Associations.*

A Union?

Examples: Teamsters, Letter Carriers, Chemical Workers, Postal Workers, Hotel and Restaurant Employees, Garment Workers, Hospital & Health Care Employees, Seafarers, Transport Workers, etc. Request the *AFL-CIO Guide to Union Sponsored Scholarships, Awards, and Student Financial Aid.* $3.00 from AFL-CIO Publications Office, 815 16th Street, NW, Rm. 209, Washington, DC 20006.

Chapter 17
Money from Your Affiliations

Your background, employment record, clubs, associations, religion and nationality may be the key to financial opportunity. Here, as in the previous chapter, you will have to develop a systematic search strategy. The matrix below will help you get started.

THE STUDENT'S MATRIX

Q. Does any job I ever held lead to a financial aid award? (Rule out babysitting for grouchy Mrs. Grumpelstein).
A. Check with the personnel office of your present or former employers.

Q. How about my clubs?
A. Check with chapter/club president or faculty adviser.

Q. What about my religious affiliation? Does my denomination sponsor student aid awards?
A. See your minister, priest, or rabbi or write to the national organizations sponsored by the denomination. Addresses in Gale's *Encyclopedia of Associations* in the reference room of the public library.

Q. How about my ancestry or my nationality?
A. Write to the organizations serving your ancestry or your nationality. Addresses in Gale's *Encyclopedia of Associations*.

What will you find? You can strike pay dirt or you can strike out. But even if you have found nothing, there is a reward. You will have learned something about research methods and become reacquainted with the public library which had greatly missed your patronage.

EXAMPLES: JOBS YOU HAVE HELD

Fast Food Worker
Burger King offers scholarships to its employees and dependents. Up to $2,000. Also minority and graduate scholarships, fellowships. Applications from your local Burger King, or from the Burger King Corporation, PO Box 520783, Miami, FL 33152. By May 1.

Golf Course Caddie
Evans Scholars Foundation. About 200 caddies receive full-tuition and housing scholarships each year. Awards are renewable for 4 years and go to students requiring financial assistance. Also, candidates must be in the top 25% of their HS class and have caddied for at least 2 years at a WGA member club. For information write Western Golf Association, Evans Scholar Foundation, Golf, IL 60029.

Newspaper Carrier
Thomas Ewing Education Grants for HS seniors who have been Washington Post carriers for at least two years; 36 awards ranging from $1000-$2000. By Jan 31. Other newspapers have similar scholarships for their carriers.

EXAMPLES: CLUBS

Boy Scouts
Directory of Scholarships and Loan Funds, a free booklet, lists programs open to scouts and former scouts. Send 9 x 12, self-addressed, stamped (2 first class stamps) envelope to: Education Relationship Services, Boy Scouts of America, 1325 Walnut Hill Lane, Irving, TX 75015.

DECA
Must be member of high school Distributive Education Club of America chapter. Other requirements: financial need; interest in a major in marketing or distribution. Information from chapter advisor.

4-H Clubs & Future Homemakers of America (FHA)
Extensive program for members. 4-H Clubs, for instance, made 287 awards worth $265,000 last year. Contact State Leader (4-H) or State Advisor (FHA).

EXAMPLES: ANCESTRY AND NATIONALITY

NSDAR
Scholarship to children of DAR members who are graduating seniors from an accredited high school. $1,000 annually for 4 years with annual transcript review. Outstanding students may renew for up to an additional 4 years. Applications to National Chairman, DAR Scholarship Committee, Mrs. R. J. Seifert, 4692 Cypress Drive, Brunswick, OH 44212. By Feb. 20.

Descendants of Signers of Declaration of Independence
Must provide definitive proof of direct lineal descent to a signer of the Declaration of Independence to the Society's Registrar-General, and be a full-time student. Requests not naming an ancestor signer will not receive a reply. 5-8 grants totaling $10,000 to $11,000, averaging $2,000. Before March 15. Contact Mr. Frederick W. Pyne, 7997 Windsail Court, Frederick, MD 21701. Or call 301-695-3935.

Italian
UNICO National, 72 Burroughs Place, Bloomfield, NJ 07003. Applicant must reside in community with UNICO chapter. By April 15.

Japanese
Japanese American Citizens League, 1765 Sutter Street, San Francisco, CA 94115. Apply by April 1. Undergraduate, graduate. Performing arts, creative arts, law, banking, business, judo.

Polish
Grants Office, The Kosciuszko Foundation, 15 East 65th Street, New York, NY 10021-6595. Polish Studies, music, voice, and others. Mainly specialized, graduate and postgrad study awards. Domestic deadline Jan. 15. Exchange program deadline Nov. 15. Summer Session in Poland (March 15 deadline).

Membership Organizations
Chinese-American Foundation, Danish Brotherhood of America, Lithuanian Alliance, Polish Falcons, Daughters of Penelope, Order of AHEPA, Sons of Norway, Sons of Poland, Russian Brotherhood Organization, Many others. Addresses of all these organizations may be found in Gale's *Encyclopedia of Associations*.

EXAMPLES: DENOMINATION

Catholic

The Pro Deo and Pro Patria scholarships. Twelve awards of $1,000. Father must be member of Knights of Columbus. Must be used at a Catholic college. Application by March 1. Also sponsors other scholarships, fellowships, graduate programs, student loans. Also awards for study in Canada, Mexico, Philippines, Puerto Rico. Contact Director of Scholarship Aid, Knights of Columbus, PO Drawer 1670, New Haven, CT 06507. Or call, 203-772-2130 x224.

Christian Scientist

Loan program. Range $1,200-$2,000 per academic year. Interest is 3% below prime during repayment which starts after graduation. Loans are interest-free to Christian Scientist nurses if they graduate. The Albert Baker Fund, 5 Third Street, Suite 717, San Francisco, CA 94103. By July 1. 703 Market Street, Suite 350, San Francisco, CA 94103. By July 1.

Jewish

Up to $7,500/year for 2 years. Graduate students preparing for careers in Jewish Community Center work. Write Scholarship Coordinator, JCC Association, 15 East 26th Street, New York, NY 10010. By Feb. 1.

Lutheran

Aid Association for Lutherans

Two competitive programs (1) All College Scholarship Program which offers 775 renewable and nonrenewable awards each year, value range: $500-$2,000. (2) Vocational-Technical School Scholarship program, 50 renewable awards each year to graduating high school seniors and 50 renewable awards each year to previous high school graduates or those with a GED: value range is $500 per year, up to a maximum of 2 years for full-time study and $250 per year, up to a maximum of 4 years for half-time study. Membership in Aid Association for Lutherans is a must. Apply by Nov. 30 to AAL, Scholarships, 4321 North Ballard Road, Appleton, WI 54915-9934.

One non-competitive program: AAL Lutheran Campus Scholarship. Membership in AAL a must. Awards made by schools. School list may be obtained from above address. From $200-$1,000/year.

Lutheran Brotherhood

Approximately 500 Member Scholarships (value to $2,000). Must be member of Lutheran Brotherhood. By Feb. 15 to Scholarship & Loan Coordinator, Lutheran Brotherhood, 625 4th Avenue South, Minneapolis, MN 55415.

Approximately 500 awards (range $800 to $1,500) to Lutheran students who attend Lutheran junior and senior colleges. Selections made by schools. Awardees do not have to be members of Lutheran Brotherhood. Also a Stafford Student Loan Program Lender.

Methodist

Grad Loans $1,200 per year; in Undergraduate non-United Methodist schools, $900 per year; in colleges affiliated with United Methodist church $1,000 per year. 6% interest. Repayment starts 6 months after graduation. Also, scholarships. Must be an active, full member of the United Methodist Church for at least one year prior to submitting application. Write to: Student Loans & Scholarships, The United Methodist Church, Board of Higher Education and Ministry, PO Box 871, Nashville, TN 37202.

Presbyterian

Scholarships from $100 to $2,000. Undergraduate and graduate. Also grants, loans, and special minority awards. Manager, Financial Aid for Studies, United Presbyterian Church in the USA, 100 Witherspoon St., Louisville, KY 40202-1396.

Chapter 18
Money Because You Have Brains and Talents

The SAT has become a national industry. The money spent on designing tests, administering tests, scoring tests, taking tests, teaching tests, coaching tests, disseminating test results, selling the names and scores of test takers to eager college recruiters, interpreting scores, analyzing scores, publicizing scores, and writing about the test, pro and con, places the SAT somewhat below the manufacture of automobiles but far ahead of the value of the horseradish crop as a contributor to our gross national product.

On the basis of all evidence, this testmania has no rational underpinnings. It is a modern addendum to the classic treatise "Popular Delusions and the Madness of Crowd." For the SAT is not an intelligence measure. It is not an aptitude measure. It is not a predictor of academic success. And getting high scores on it isn't always important for gaining college admission. It's only verifiable characteristics are that, one, it corresponds quite closely to family income. The higher the income, the higher the scores. And two, it thrives on criticism. The more it is attacked and exposed, the more it gains in universality and acceptance.

But this outburst should not turn you away from the test. High scores have a direct monetary application. They can cost you money or they can make money for you.

Cost you money? you ask. How? Suppose you live in a school district which emphasizes test coaching and test teaching. That emphasis will raise scores. And higher scores cause property values to soar because parents from everywhere now want to move into your district so that the smarts rub off on junior. Your $50,000 home with a swampy basement, shaky foundation, and a resident population of overweight termite gourmets is suddenly worth $100,000, a nice increase that adds $2,500 to your family contribution. Frankly, we have never understood why enterprising real estate firms don't underwrite SAT preparation courses. It could be their "smartest investment."

Now that we have learned how the SAT can cost you money, let's see how it can make you money. Here is what good scores can do:

1. Qualify you for a National Merit or Regent Scholarship (recent court cases notwithstanding).
2. Push you over the eligibility cut-off line of thousands of academic scholarships offered by colleges.
3. Give you bargaining power when negotiating the content of a financial aid package. Your higher scores make you more valuable to the school because they help raise the average for the entire entering freshman class.

The hard way to raise SAT scores is to find an error in the test and appeal it. The easier way is to take a good SAT preparation course—but take it for the practical reasons listed above and not for any mythological reasons.

If a $500 investment in a SAT preparation course can yield a $2,000 no-need scholarship, renewed each year for four years, you have done far better with your money than the shrewdest Wall Street stock picker.

A good organization with a successful track record for raising SAT scores is Stanley Kaplan, Ltd. Call 1-800-KAPTEST; in New York (212) 977-8687 for the location of the nearest test center.

WHERE ARE THE REWARDS FOR THE BRIGHT?

The best listing is in *The A's & B's of Academic Scholarships* (see inside back cover). It describes the 100,000 academic awards offered at 1200 colleges; awards that range in value from $200 to $20,000 per year. Most of these awards, moreover, are not based on financial need.

DO YOU HAVE BRAINS, LEADERSHIP, TALENT?

Many scholarship opportunities are reserved for young people with unusual talents and abilities. There are two major ways of linking up with these opportunities: (1) through competitions; and (2) through recommendations of teachers, coaches, bandmasters.

Art

Scholastic Art Awards. Cash, scholarships, other. Grades 7-12. Scholastic, Inc., 730 Broadway, New York, NY 10003.

Arts (Dance, Music, Theater, Visual Arts, Writing)

Scholarships, cash awards, apprenticeships, identification of talented students to colleges who may offer additional awards to prospects. HS seniors or those 17 or 18 years of age by Dec. 1 the year they apply. $35.00 registration fee. Arts Recognition & Talent Search, 300 NE 2nd Avenue, Miami, FL 33132. By Oct. 1. (305) 347-3416.

Brains

1. *National Merit Scholarship Corporation.* Participants take the PSAT/NMSQT. Finalists compete for c. 1800 non-renewable $2,000 scholarships and c. 4200 renewable scholarships (worth from $250 to $2,000+ per year). Obtain Student Bulletin from National Merit Scholarship Corporation, 1560 Sherman Ave., Suite 200, Evanston, IL 60201-4897.
2. *National Honor Society.* 250 $1,000 scholarships for members of the National Honor Society. Nominations through HS chapter. February deadline.
3. *Mensa Scholarships.* Awards to $1,000. Based on essay competition. Application from local Mensa group with self-addressed stamped envelope, by January 31.

Citizenship

HS seniors. Entries judged on basis of an application. (1) $1,250 award per Soroptimist region and (1) $2,500 finalist award. Deadline December 15. Contact your local Soroptimist Club.

Drama

Thespian Society (majors in theater arts). Members only scholarships. Through HS chapter.

General

Approved list of contests. Ask for Advisory List of National Contests and Activities $4.00, National Association of Secondary School Principals, 1904 Association Dr., Reston, VA 22091.

Leadership & Brains

1. *Josten Foundation.* Nonrenewable awards (200 $500) to recognize outstanding high school seniors. Program is administered by Citizens Scholarship Foundation, Josten Foundation National Scholarship, PO Box 297, St. Peter, MN 56082. Announcement and guidelines sent to high schools in September. November 15 deadline.
2. *Shell Century III Leaders Scholarship Program.* National winner: $11,500; Nine $2,000 runner-ups. Also two primary winners per state—$1,500 each—and two state alternates $500 each. Program is administered by National Association of Secondary School Principals. Program announcement placed in high schools in September. October deadline. Seniors only.

3. *Principal's Leadership Award (PLA)*. 150 $1,000 scholarships. Applications sent to high school principal in October. December deadline. Seniors only. Program is administered by National Association of Secondary School Principals.
4. *U. S. Senate Youth Program*. 104 $2,000 scholarships to elected student government officers. Selections by state. William Randolph Hearst Foundation, 90 New Montgomery St., #1212, San Francisco, CA 94105. (415) 543-4057.
5. *Truman Scholars*. $30,000 max. over 4 years. 92 awards. Nominated by colleges in sophomore or junior year. Awards are for junior or senior year plus up to 3 years of graduate school. Solid class standing. Outstanding potential for leadership in the public service. Harry S. Truman Scholarship Foundation, 712 Jackson Place, NW, Washington, DC 20006. Nominations by December 1.

Math and Natural Sciences

Barry M. Goldwater Scholarship. Undergraduate scholarships to outstanding college sophomores and juniors who plan to pursue careers in math and natural sciences. Tuition, fees, books, room and board, up to $7,000/year for 2 years. One scholarship to a resident of each state. Additional scholars-at-large may also be chosen (245 scholarships were awarded last year). Applicants are selected and nominated by their college. By January 31. Contact Barry M. Goldwater Scholarship & Excellence in Education Foundation, 499 S. Capitol Street, SW, Suite 405, Washington, DC, 20003-4013. (202) 755-2312.

Math, Science and Computer Science

Tandy Technology Scholars. 100 awards of $1,000 each. Final selection based on GPA, SAT/ACT scores, excellence in math, science or computer science, and service to the community. Nominated by HS. For more information, write Tandy Technology Scholars, PO Box 32897, TCU Station, Fort Worth, TX 76129.

Oratory & Essays

Many contests. American Legion, Optimist International, Civitan.

Photography

Scholastic Photography Awards. Cash, scholarships, other. Grades 7-12. Scholastic, Inc., 730 Broadway, New York, NY 10003.

Political Science

First Nationwide Network Scholarship Program. 32 awards of $1,000 each to college juniors majoring in political science, history, or government. Established to honor John F. Kennedy. Essay and application required. Call First Nationwide Network program manager at 507-931-1682 for more information.

Presidential Scholars

No application. No nomination. Approximately 120 students selected from high scorers on the SAT and ACT. Also 20 students picked for achievement in the arts, as identified by the Arts Recognition & Talent Search (see above). A four-day visit to Washington. A handshake from the President. And $1,000 from the Dodge Foundation.

Science

Westinghouse Science Talent Search Scholarships. Students in the last year of secondary school may enter the competition by submitting a report on an independent research project in science, mathematics, or engineering, along with standardized test scores, transcript and application. Applications must be requested by a HS official and mailed to the school address. $205,000 in scholarships, ranging from $40,000 to $1,000. Deadline for entries is early December. Contact Science Service, 1719 N Street, NW, Washington, DC 20036. (202) 785-2255.

The Unusual?

Can you do bagpipes, Scottish drums or highland flings? Arkansas College has some scholarships for you. Change your kilt for jeans, hop on a Brahma bull, and the National HS Rodeo Association (12200 Pecos Street, Suite 250, Denver, CO 80234) can present you with a $1,500 rodeo scholarship.

Writing

1. *Scholastic Writing Awards.* Cash, scholarships, other. Grades 7-12. Scholastic, Inc., 730 Broadway, New York, NY 10003.
2. *Youth Writing Contest.* High School seniors. (1) $6,000; (1) $5,000; (1) $4,000; (1) $3,000; (1) $2,000; and (5) $1,000 scholarships. Electronic typewriters to the top 30 finishers. Write and submit a first person, 1200 word story about a memorable or moving experience you have had, preferably spiritual. Deadline November 28. GuidePosts, 747 Third Avenue, New York, NY 40017.

Chapter 19
Money Because You Are an Athlete

A SUMMARY

Athletic scholarships are not limited to those with prowess in the big sports—football, baseball, basketball, hockey, soccer, tennis, and track. There is scholarship money for sailing, badminton, gymnastics, lacrosse, bowling, archery, fencing, rowing, synchronized swimming, skiing and volleyball.

All-star athletes don't need this book. They need an agent who can sort through the offers, enticements, contracts and gifts that come their way. They might need a mechanic, too, to advise them on the relative merits of a Porsche or a Mercedes.

This chapter is for the better-than-average athlete with varsity potential in major and minor sports. What's available for this athlete? How do you link up with it?

Here is the situation in a nutshell:

There is considerable financial aid available at most colleges for students who also happen to be good, but not necessarily great, athletes. This aid is either "reserved" for athletes (through designated scholarships) or awarded on a preferential basis as part of the financial aid packaging process.

The key to receiving consideration for this kind of aid lies in the student athlete's determination to market his or her talents. This marketing procedure is based on contacting the appropriate coach at the desired college and getting that coach to shepherd the student's request for admission and financial aid through the bureaucracy of the various institutional admissions and financial aid offices. All college coaches, if convinced of the student athlete's potential contribution to their sport, will take an active role in facilitating the student's admission and financial requests.

For example, some schools have admission representatives whose main responsibility is to coordinate referrals from the athletic department.

Here is a step-by-step outline that students should follow in marketing their athletic talents:

1. Discuss with your guidance counselor the range of colleges for which you are academically qualified. In selecting suitable schools, keep in mind that approximately 20% of all colleges will reconsider their admission standards to "land" an athlete.
2. Talk to your high school coach about the range and quality of college athletic programs for which you might qualify. Don't sell yourself short. Coaches not only need first stringers but also back-up players.
3. Narrow your college selection list to a manageable size, taking into consideration the quality of athletic and academic programs and your "fit" with them. In other words, you *don't* want to be a four-year bench-warmer; you *do* want to be challenged by the school's academic program (but not over- or underwhelmed).
4. Research the name of the coach in your sport at each college on your list. Best source: your high school athletic director's copy of *The National Directory of College Athletics* (there are separate editions of this book for men and women).
5. Draft a personal letter to each coach. This letter should include a profile of your academic interests and achievements. The letter's main part, however, should be a thorough and detailed discussion of your athletic accomplishments and be supported by statistics, clippings, letters earned, records, and honors. Include mention of any camps or clinics you've attended, and where appropriate, send a videotape of you in action! Lastly, indicate you will require financial aid.

6. If your approach elicits interest on the part of the colleges, ask the high school coach to follow up with either a letter of recommendation or a phone call. You may also want to send the college a copy of your scheduled games in case recruiters are in the area!
7. Now you must decide where to apply. Few college coaches will take an interest in you unless your initial letter is followed by a formal application. And remember: here, as with any other application, apply as early as possible.
8. After applying, remain in touch with the college coaches. Inquire about the status of your application and request for financial aid. If possible, visit the college and the coach and sell yourself as a person and as an athlete. Get to know the coach, and make certain his or her coaching philosophy is compatible with style!

QUESTIONS & ANSWERS

Q. What do you think of commercial athletic scholarship services?
A. There are numerous services that represent the student in the search for athletic scholarships. Their fee normally runs $250 or higher, plus, where it is not prohibited, a percentage of the first year's award. The services generally follow the eight steps outlined above. There is no reason why you shouldn't "sell" yourself and save the services' fee.

Q. What is better? Preferential packaging of the aid award or an athletic scholarship?
A. Preferential packaging. If you have a personality conflict with the coach or run into a physical problem that keeps you from competing, you can lose your scholarship. The financial aid package, once it is wrapped up, will hold for a year.

Q. Do you recommend any references for further reading?
A. Yes. The National Collegiate Athletic Association (NCAA) publishes stiff rules on the do's and don'ts of recruiting athletes. Get *The NCAA Guide for the College-Bound Student* from NCAA Publishing, 6201 College Boulevard, Overland Park, Kansas 66211-2422. The brochures are sold in bundles of 50, but you may be able to get a single copy for free.

Q. Are college athletic programs really in need of major clean-up?
A. Don't let headlines scare you. Most of the abuses you read about, while extremely serious, are restricted to the big name football and basketball programs. The fact is, students who compete in collegiate athletic programs have a higher graduation rate than other students and fare better economically in the job market.

Q. Anything else?
A. Be sure to locate a copy of *The National Directory of College Athletics* for the names of college coaches. Also, get a copy of *The Winning Edge: The Student-Athlete's Guide to College Sports* ($7.50, postpaid) from Octameron Associates. It provides a detailed strategy for taking your sport to college, as well as advice from actual coaches on maximizing your chances for scholarship assistance..

Q. How can I tell which colleges offer scholarships and in what sports?
A. Check the high school guidance office for a copy of *Lovejoy's College Guide*. It lists colleges that offer sports scholarships (broken down by sport). Women should also get *The Women's Athletic Scholarship Guide* from the Women's Sports Foundation, 342 Madison Avenue, Suite 728, New York, NY 10173; 212-972-9170 or 800-227-3988.

Chapter 20
Money for Health Careers

As a budding nurse or doctor or therapist, don't limit your reading to this chapter. Or you will never blossom out into a nurse or doctor or therapist.

You'll find other money sources in different parts of this book. For instance, all the major federal student aid programs (in Chapter 10) will help pay for your medical education. Many of the states (Chapter 11) furnish help in those medical fields in which they believe they have shortages. And there is support for minority medical education. It's described in Chapter 22.

Finally, *College Loans From Uncle Sam* (see inside back cover) goes into all the ins and outs of the major medical loan programs.

FEDERAL SUPPORT FOR THE HEALTH PROFESSIONS

Uncle Sam pours great amounts of money—almost one half a billion dollars per year—into the training of health professionals. The assistance programs fall into two broad categories; those that fund students and those that fund schools which then parcel out some of their money to students.

The individual-based programs are fairly easy to locate. You apply directly to Uncle Sam or through the school you plan to attend. One bit of advice we can give you: You will gain an advantage over fellow applicants if you indicate a willingness to practice your profession in a shortage area. Don't worry about what a shortage area is. Its definition and location will change several times between the time you apply and the time you graduate. What's important to know is that "shortage areas" are a big thing in the operation of the Department of Health & Human Services. It has "primary medical care shortage areas," "dental manpower shortage areas," "rural dental shortage areas," "vision care shortage areas," "podiatry shortage areas," "pharmacy shortage areas," "psychiatric shortage areas," even "veterinary care shortage areas." Can you say "Northern Exposure"?

School-based programs are something else. Here, Uncle demonstrates the technique of buying horses to feed sparrows. The available dollars go directly to schools and usually become part of the faculty payroll (the reason: Medical faculties are high-priced; without federal aid to help pay their salaries, the schools would have to foot the bill alone. To do this, the schools would have to raise tuition so high that no student could afford to enroll). Your challenge is to locate the schools which garnered Uncle's grants and negotiate with deans for some of the lavishings. When writing to the addresses given in the tables that follow, be sure to ask for a current list of funded schools—and be aggressive in your request. The program officers with whom you will deal usually won't understand why you need this information. They think in terms of institutions, not students. You'll have to be polite but tough and persistent.

To save space, we have used the following coding to denote medical fields. Check the coding before entering the table.

```
A—Allied Health, MA or higher      I—Nursing, Advanced
B—Chiropractic                     J—Nursing, Anesthetist
C—Dentistry                        K—Nursing, Community Health
D—Health Administration            L—Nursing, Midwifery
E—Medicine                         M—Nursing, Psychiatric
F—Nursing, Associate               N—Nutrition
G—Nursing, Diploma                 O—Optometry
H—Nursing, Baccalaureate           P—Osteopathy
```

Q—Pharmacy
R—Podiatry
S—Psychology, Clinical
T—Public Health, MA or higher
U—Safety, Occupational
V—Social Work
W—Therapy, Occupational
X—Therapy, Physical
Y—Therapy, Rehabilitation
Z—Veterinary Medicine

INDIVIDUAL-BASED PROGRAMS

A-B-C-D-E-O-P-Q-R-S-T-Z. Health Education Assistance Loans. Medical, Dental, Osteopathic, Optometry, Podiatry, and Veterinary Medicine students may borrow $20,000 per year for total of $80,000. Other students: $12,500 per year (limit $50,000). Floating interest rate (91-day Treasury Bill average plus 3%). Includes Graduate students. Program is not authorized for study at foreign medical schools. Apply through school or write: HEAL, Room 8-38, 5600 Fishers Lane, Rockville, MD 20857.

C-E-O-P-Q-R-T-Z. Health Professions Student Loan. Tuition plus $2,500 per year. 9% interest. Must show great financial need. Uncle will repay a good part of loan if you elect to practice in a shortage area following graduation. Apply through school.

E-F-G-H-I-J-K-L-P. National Health Service Corp Loan Repayment Program. In return for a 2-year minimum, full-time practice in a specified shortage area, the NHSC will pay up to $35,000/year toward a participant's outstanding government and commercial education loans; NHSC Loan Repayment Info, DHSS, Rm. 7-18, Parklawn Bldg., 5600 Fishers Lane, Rockville, MD 20857.

C-E-I-J-K-L-O-P-Q-R-Z. National Health Service Corp Scholarship Program. The NHSC will pay tuition, fees, books and supplies, plus a monthly stipend of $736 for up to four years. For each year of support, award recipients owe one year of full-time clinical practice in high-priority health professions shortage areas. For more information, write: NHSC Scholarship Program, DHSS, Rm. 7-18, Parklawn Bldg., 5600 Fishers Lane, Rockville, MD 20857.

C-E-O-P-Q-R-Z. Exceptional Need Scholarships. All tuition plus stipend. Good for one year only. At completion of year, participants have priority for a NHSC Scholarship. Apply through school.

F-G-H-I-J-K-L-M-W-X-Y. Veterans Affairs Scholarship Program. Scholarships available to second (final) year students in NLN accredited associate degree nursing programs, and upper division baccalaureate or master's degree students in accredited (NLN) nursing, (AOTA) occupational therapy and (APTA) physical therapy programs, on a competitive basis. Benefits include full tuition and fees, monthly stipends and other educational costs. In return for benefits, participants work full-time as professionals in VA medical centers one year for every year or part of a year benefits are provided. Applications available March through May from Deans/Directors and Financial Aid Administrators of accredited schools, Chiefs of Nursing or Rehabilitation Medicine at any VA medical center, or Department of Veterans Affairs, Health Professional Scholarship Program (143C2), 810 Vermont Avenue, NW, Washington, DC 20420. (202) 535-7527. Deadline to receive completed applications is May 29.

F-G-H-I. Nursing Student Loan Program. Up to $2,500 per year to maximum of $10,000. Need. 6% interest. Apply through school.

All Health Related Fields. Commissioned Officer Student Training & Extern Program (COSTEP) Work Program. For graduate awards, students must have completed minimum of 1 yr. graduate work in medical, dental, veterinary school. For undergraduate awards, students must have completed 2 yrs in a dietary, nursing, pharmacy, therapy, sanitary science, medical records, engineering, physician's assistant, or computer science field. For other areas, students must be enrolled in master's or doctoral program. Student must return to studies following completion of the COSTEP assignment. Serve as an extern (another word for intern) in medical facilities of the Public Health Service during school breaks of 31-120 days duration. Get ensign's pay during work phases. Send for more information. COSTEP, Room 4A-07, Parklawn Bldg., 5600 Fishers Lane, Rockville, MD 20857.(301) 443-6324.

I-S-W-X-Y. Rehabilitation Training. Monthly trainee stipends. When inquiring, refer to Program 84.129. (Rehab Counseling, Physical and Occupational Therapy, Prosthetics-Orthotics, Speech Language-Pathology, Audiology, Rehab Services to the Blind and Deaf). Employment obligation or payback provisions govern rehabilitation long-term training scholarships. Department of Education, Rehabilitation Services Administration, 400 Maryland Avenue, SW, Washington, DC 20202.

SCHOOL-BASED PROGRAMS

I-J-K-L. Traineeships for Advanced Education of Professional Nurses. Nurse practitioners, nurse administrators, nurse educators, nurse midwifery, nurse anesthetist, nurse researchers, and other nursing specialties. Tuition, fees, and stipends. Funded through participating schools (most graduate nursing programs participate). Division of Nursing, Room 5C26, 5600 Fishers Lane, Rockville, MD 20857.

D-T. (1) Traineeships in Graduate Programs of Health Administration; (2) Graduate Level Public Health Traineeships. Annual stipends and/or tuition assistance, awarded by the educational institution receiving a grant. Division of Associated and Dental Health Professions, HRSA, 5600 Fishers Lane, Rm. 8C-09, Rockville, MD 20857.

M-S-V. Mental Health Research (biomedical and behavioral). National Research Service awards for individual fellows (pre- and post-doctoral). Pre-doctoral stipend, $8,500. Post-doctoral stipend is determined by years of experience. Range is $17,000 to $31,500. Grants Management Branch—National Institute of Mental Health, 5600 Fishers Lane, Rm. 7C-15, Rockville, MD 20857.

V. Child Welfare Training Grants. Undergraduate and graduate social work programs or child welfare training programs. Awarded by school. Children's Bureau, PO Box 1182, Washington, DC 20013.

U. Occupational Safety & Health Training Grants. Paraprofessional, undergraduate and graduate level. Refer to Program 13.263 (mostly graduate level). Public Health Service, 5600 Fishers Lane, Rockville, MD 20857.

MILITARY MEDICAL AND NURSING PROGRAMS

Uniformed Services University of the Health Sciences (USUHS)

The F. Edward Hebert School of Medicine. USUHS is a tuition-free, four-year medical school. Students receive the salary of an O-1 officer. Additional military service is required after all medical training. 162 openings per year. Admissions, USUHS, 4301 Jones Bridge Rd., Bethesda, MD 20814-4799; 1-800-772-1743.

Armed Forces Health Professions Scholarship Program

Medicine, optometry, nurse anesthesia (Masters degree). Generous monthly stipend plus tuition, fees and books, lab expenses, educational services. Service obligation. Ask for scholarship fact sheet from Assistant Secretary of Defense (Health Affairs), The Pentagon, Washington, D C. 20301-1200.

Armed Forces Health Professions Financial Assistance Program

Specialized (residency) training for graduate physicians. Annual $15,000 grant plus generous monthly stipend and educational expenses. Service obligation. Each branch of the service has its own point of contact. Write for fact sheets:

Army	Navy	Air Force
Col. R. T. Maruka	Capt. B. T. Hogan	Directorate of Health Professionals
HQ, DA (SGPS-PDO)	Medical Command, US Navy	HQ, USAF Recruiting Service
5109 Leesburg Pike, #638	BUMED	Randolph AFB, TX 76150
Falls Church, VA 22041	Washington, DC 20372-5120	800-531-5980
703-756-8114	202-653-5980	

ROTC Nurse Program (Army, Navy, Air Force)

Students at an approved nursing school affiliated with an Army, Navy, or Air Force ROTC unit. 2, 3, 4 year scholarships; tuition, textbooks, and fees, plus $100/month (Although Army ROTC Scholarships are limited to 80% of tuition or $7,500/yr., whichever is larger). Service obligation. Air Force also offers 1 year, 2 1/2, and 3 1/2 year scholarships.

Army	Navy	Air Force
Army ROTC	Commander	HQ AFROTC
Attn: ATCC-N	Navy Recruiting Command	Recruiting Division
Ft. Monroe, VA 23651	(Code 314)	Maxwell AFB, AL 36112
800-USA-ROTC	4015 Wilson Blvd.	
	Arlington, VA 22203-1991	
	703-696-4581	

AF ROTC Pre-Health Professions Program

Premedicine. Attend a school offering AF ROTC. 2 and 3 year scholarships. Tuition, textbooks, fees, plus $100/month. Service obligation. HQ AFROTC Recruiting Division, Maxwell AFB, AL 36112-6663.

PRIVATE PROGRAMS

Blood Technology

5 $1,500 awards annually. Accepted or enrolled in accredited program leading to specialist in blood banking certification. AABB, Suite 600, 1117 N. 19th St., Arlington, VA 22209. By April 1.

Dental Assistant

Student Scholarship. $100/$1,000. Juliett A. Southard Scholarship Trust Fund, American Dental Assistants Association, 919 N. Michigan Avenue, Suite 3400, Chicago, IL 60611.

Dental Hygienist

AA, BA, MA, Ph.D. awards to students enrolled in at least second year of dental hygiene program. To $1,500. Also minority program. ADHA Institute for Oral Health, 444 N. Michigan, #3400, Chicago, IL 60611. By May 1.

Dental Lab Technology

15-20 scholarships per year. $500 to $600 for students enrolled or planning to enroll in accredited Dental Administration or DLT program. 1st or 2nd year of study; engage in DLT for 3 years. By June 1. American Fund for Dental Health, 211 E. Chicago Ave., Suite 820, Chicago, IL 60611.

Nursing

Information on scholarships, loans, grants, fellowships, awards. Send $14.45 (postpaid) for the book *Scholarships and Loans for Nursing Education*, Publication No. 41-1964; pre-payment must accompany order. National League for Nursing, 350 Hudson St., New York, NY 10014.

Nursing (Advanced)

Scholarship for registered nurses, members of a national, professional nursing association, for advanced degrees. Masters and doctoral. $2,500-$10,000. Full-time student at master's level, full-time or part-time at doctoral level. By Feb. 1. Nurses' Educational Funds, Inc., 555 W. 57th St., 13th Floor, New York, NY 10019.

Laboratory
Several scholarships to help obtain an education in medical lab technology. Limited to International Society for Clinical Laboratory Technology members, or their children. ISCLT Scholarship Committee, 818 Olive St., #918, St. Louis, MO 63101.

Surgical Technology
One $500 award with others possible. For students in CAHEA-accredited surgical technology program. Association of Surgical Technologists, 8307 Shaffer Parkway, Littleton, CO 80127. By March 1.

Therapy (All)
Several $750/$1,000 undergraduate and graduate awards. U.S. or Canadian resident, completed 2 yrs. of undergrad study on a campus where a chapter of Kappa Kappa Gamma is located. Ask your local chapter head for more information.

Therapy (Occupational)
1. Undergraduate and Graduate awards, grants, fellowships. AOT Foundation, Inc., 1383 Piccard Dr., Rockville, MD 20850. By Dec. 15.
2. Occupational Therapy scholarships. To students enrolled in accredited school of Occupational Therapy (physical, art, music). Number and amounts vary. Applications to National Chairman, DAR Scholarship Committee, Mrs. R. J. Seifert, 4692 Cypress Drive, Brunswick, OH 44212. By September 1. No affiliation or relationship with DAR necessary.

Therapy (Physical, Occupational, Music, Speech)
500 awards per year, $500-$1,500 junior/senior undergraduate and graduate scholarships. National AMBUCS Scholarships for Therapists, P.O. Box 5127, High Point, NC 27262. Deadline is May 1.

Therapy (Respiratory)
Various scholarships and awards, $500-$1,250. American Respiratory Care Foundation, 11030 Ables Lane, Dallas, TX 75229. By June 1.

Chapter 21
Money for Other Career Interests

The best way to capitalize on your career interest is through cooperative education (Chapter 12). The next best way is to enroll in a school with a strong reputation in your career field (e.g., Agriculture—*Iowa State*; Hotel Management—*Cornell*). Strong departments usually attract scholarship funds. These funds, however, do not start flowing until you declare your major. The third—and hardest method—is to look for portable scholarships that will fund your major at any accredited school. The list that follows is illustrative, rather than complete. To dig for additional awards, contact (1) the organizations that provide career information in your field of interest (you'll find them in *Need a Lift?*) and (2) the professional associations which serve these careers (locate those in Volume 1, Gale's *Encyclopedia of Associations*). When writing, always enclose a self-addressed, stamped business-size envelope (SASE).

Accounting
1. National Society of Public Accountants. 22 $1,000 awards; 1 $2,000 award. Undergraduates only. B average in accounting subjects. Deadline March 20. National Society of Public Accountants Scholarship Foundation, 1010 N. Fairfax St., Alexandria, VA 22314.
2. Robert Kaufman Memorial Scholarships. Up to 20 awards, ranging from $250 to $5000. Undergraduates who plan to pursue an education in accounting can get more information from the Independent Accountants International Education Fund, 9200 South Dadeland Blvd., Suite 510, Miami, FL 33156; or call 305-661-3580. By 28 February.

Architecture
American Inst. of Architects offers undergrad and grad scholarships/awards. Undergrad applications through office of the head of an accredited school or its scholarship committee. From $500-$2,000. By Feb. 1. Grad and professional awards from $1,000-$2,500. No later than Feb. 15th. Contact Scholarship Programs, AIA, 1735 New York Ave., NW, Washington, DC 20006.

Art & Architecture
A full scholarship school. All admitted students receive a full scholarship for duration of their study. Dean of Admissions, Cooper Union, 41 Cooper Square, New York, NY 10003.

Art
Frances Hook Scholarship Fund Art Awards Program. Art scholarships to encourage young, talented artists. Grades 1 to college undergraduate, under 24 years of age. $250-$2,500. Artwork must be two-dimensional (no sculptures). Oil, acrylics, pencil, charcoal, pastel, water color, ink, or any combination of these mediums. No photographs. Artwork must be received Feb. 15-March 15. Contact Frances Hook Scholarship Fund, 1910 W. County Road B, Roseville, MN 55113. (612) 636-6436.

Education
41 at $1,000 and one $2,000. International grants to HS seniors planning on a teaching career. Scholarship Grants, Phi Delta Kappa, PO Box 789, Bloomington, IN 47402. January 31 deadline.

Engineering (Civil/Construction)
Various awards. 25-30 undergrad awards of $1,500/yr. for 4 years renewable. Graduate awards of up to $7,500. Director of Programs, AGC Education & Research Foundation, 1957 E St., NW, Washington, DC 20006. By November 15. (202) 393-2040.

Engineering (Materials)
31 $500 scholarships, 3 $1,000 scholarships. Students majoring in materials science and engineering (metallurgy, metallurgical engineering, ceramics, ceramics engineering, polymers, polymer engineering, composites, composite engineering). Sophomore or above (undergrad). North American (US, Canada, Mexico) citizen. ASM, Materials Park, OH 44073. By June 15.

Engineering (Mining)
100+ scholarships up to $2,000. Request Guide to Scholarships. Society for Mining, Metallurgy, and Exploration, PO Box 625002, Littleton, CO 80162-5002.

Engineering
1. *National Society of Professional Engineers.* Top 25% HS standing. US citizen. 3.0 GPA. V-500, M-600. 150 scholarships from $1,000 to $25,000. Financial need; interview. Renewable. Some reserved for minorities, women, and graduate students. NSPE Education Foundation, 1420 King St., Alexandria, VA 22314. By Nov. 15.
2. *Cooper Union.* A full scholarship school. Every admitted student receives a full scholarship for duration of study. Dean of Admission, Cooper Union, 41 Cooper Square, New York, NY 10003.

Enology & Viticulture
Several awards to graduate students and undergrads (enrolled in a 4-year degree program) majoring in enology or other science basic to the wine and grape industry. Applicants must meet minimum GPA requirements. By March 1. American Society for Enology and Viticulture, PO Box 1855, Davis, CA 95617.

Entomology
Two undergrad scholarships annually. $500 and $1,000. Major in biology, entomology, or related science at recognized school in U. S., Canada, Mexico. Min. of 30 semester hrs. accumulated. Executive Director, Education and Training Committee, ESA, 9301 Annapolis Road, Lanham, MD 20706. By May 1.

Food (Management, Dietetics, Culinary Arts, etc.)
100+ undergrad scholarships. 3.2 GPA. $500-$2,000. Betsy Schroeder, Scholarship Services, The Educational Foundation of the National Restaurant Assoc., 250 South Wacker Drive, Suite 1400, Chicago, IL 60606. (312) 715-1010. By March 1.

Food (Dairy)
Loans up to $1,500, 4% interest rate. At least 1 year of college completed. U. S. or Canadian citizen. Dairy/Food Science majors. Dairy Remembrance Fund, 6425 Executive Blvd., Rockville, MD 20852.

Food (Management)
Local branches of Association offer $100 to $500 grants. $90,000 awarded last year. International Food Service Executives Assoc., 1100 S. State Road 7, #103, Margate, FL 33068. By Feb 1.

Food (Technology)
107 undergrad and grad scholarships. $750-$10,000. Scholarship Dept., Institute of Food Technologists, 221 N. LaSalle St., #300, Chicago, IL 60601. By Feb. 1 for grad/jr. & sr. Feb. 15 for freshmen. March 1 for sophomores.

Foreign Study
1. *The Rotary Foundation.* c.1300 Scholarships. Undergraduate, graduate, vocational, teacher of handicapped, journalism. Awards: fields of peace studies, agriculture, Japanese studies. Scholarships include transportation, fees, some supplies, housing, board, travel. Contact

local Rotary Club or write: The Rotary Foundation, One Rotary Center, 1560 Sherman Ave., Evanston, IL, USA, 60201. Deadline on or before July 15.
2. *The Insider's Guide to Foreign Study by Benedict Leerburger.* Descriptions of 400 academic programs abroad, including information on admission requirements, number of credits offered, teaching methods, housing options, and costs. Not much help on financing, but otherwise valuable. $12.95. Addison-Wesley Publishing Co. (order through local bookstores).

Geology
Up to $2,000. Masters and doctoral thesis research at universities in U.S., Canada, Mexico, Central America. Members and non-members eligible. Contact Research Grants Administrator, Geological Soc. of America, PO Box 9140, Boulder, CO 80301.

Geophysics
Need and competence. 60-100 awards. Average: $1,000. Students taking course work directed toward career in Geophysics. Scholarship Committee, SEG Foundation, PO Box 702740, Tulsa, OK 74170. By March 1.

Golf Course Maintenance
Scholarship Program by Golf Course Superintendents Assoc. of America. Also a Legacy Award. Selection is based upon leadership, scholastic capabilities, character, verbal and social skills. GCSAA, 1421 Research Park, Lawrence, KS 66049, by October 1. 913-832-4470.

Graphic Arts
1. *New England Graphic Arts Scholarships.* 87 awards totaling $120,000. Given to high school students or recent graduates who intend to study the graphic arts. Must be a New England resident. New England Graphic Arts Scholarships, PO Box 1679, Boston, MA 02205.
2. *National Scholarship Trust Fund.* Scholarships, $300-$1,000. Renewable. National Scholarship Trust Fund, 4615 Forbes Ave., Pittsburgh, PA 15213. By Jan. 15.

History
National Society, Daughters of the American Revolution. $8,000/4 years. HS senior. Top third of class. Major in American History. All students are judged on the basis of academic excellence, commitment to the field of study and financial need. Send applications to the DAR Scholarship Committee State Chair by 1 Feb. One winner from each state is submitted to the National Chair. For more information, send SASE to: NSDAR, Office of the Committees, 1776 D St., NW, Washington, DC 20006. By Feb. 1.

Home Economics
National and International fellowships, awards, and grants. $1,000-$5,000. Applications from AHEA Foundation, Fellowships, Grants, Awards, 1555 King St., Alexandria, VA 22314.

Horticulture
1. *Professional Plant Growers.* $1,000-$2,000 undergraduate (Jr/Sr year) and $1,000-$2,000 graduate scholarships. Renewable. By May 1. Professional Plant Growers Scholarship Foundation, PO Box 27517, Lansing, MI 48909. (517) 694-7700. U.S. or Canadian citizen.
2. *American Orchid Society.* Grants for experimental projects and research on orchids. Also biological research, conservation, ecology. $100-$10,000. And fellowship. Up to 3 years working on orchid-related dissertation projects that lead to the Ph.D. degree. Must be enrolled full-time in a doctoral program of an accredited academic institution in the U.S. $9,000/yr. Application by Jan. 1. American Orchid Society, 6000 South Olive Ave., West Palm Beach, FL 33405.
3. *American Horticulture Society.* Paid Summer Internships for students who have obtained or are working toward undergrad degree in Horticulture or related plant science field. Write Curator, American Horticulture Society, 7931 E. Boulevard Drive, Alexandria, VA 22308.

Journalism
Excellent booklet listing $3 million in journalism scholarships. Write for Journalism Career and Scholarship Guide. Has minority section. Dow Jones Newspaper Fund, Inc., PO Box 300, Princeton, NJ 08543-0300. First copy free OR one copy free per address.

Librarianship
Compendium of scholarships available for Library Technical Assistant and Librarian. Ask for booklet Financial Assistance for Library Education, include $1.00. Standing Committee on Library Education, ALA, 50 E. Huron St., Chicago, IL 60611.

Merchant Marine
$100/month subsistence allowance for many students at California, Maine, Massachusetts, SUNY, Texas, and Great Lakes Maritime Academies. Service obligation. Academies Program Officer, Maritime Administration, 400 Seventh St., SW, Washington, DC 20590.

Music
Request Scholarship and Awards Chart, listing hundreds of opportunities. Include a large, self-addressed, (2 first class) stamped envelope. National Federation of Music Clubs Headquarters, 1336 N. Delaware St., Indianapolis, IN 46202.

Naval Architecture
Ship design. All tuition paid. Top students. High SAT. Webb Institute of Naval Architecture, Crescent Beach Rd., Glen Cove, NY 11542-1398.

Private Club Management
Scholarships. Apply after first year of college. Essay, 2.5 GPA required. Club Managers Association of America, 1733 King St., Alexandria, VA 22314. By May 1.

Public Service
$500 and $1,000 awards. Careers in Government service. Public Employees Roundtable scholarships. Undergrad and graduate level. Must be working toward degree, 3.5 GPA. Must plan to pursue career in Government. Contact congressional representative or PER, PO Box 6184, Ben Franklin Station, Washington, DC 20044-6184, or (202) 535-4324. By May 21.

Real Estate Appraisers
50 scholarships. $3,000/grad. students, $2,000/undergraduates. American Inst. of Real Estate Appraisers, 430 N. Michigan, Chicago, IL 60611. By March 15.

Science and Engineering
Bell & Howell Scholarships. Electronics, engineering technology, computer science, business. Scores, transcript. 60 $11,000 scholarships ($2,750/yr. for 4 years). Bell & Howell Education Group, Inc., B & H Science & Engineering Scholarship, 2201 W. Howard St., Evanston, IL 60202. (708) 328-8100 or 1-800-225-8000.

Special Education
Career preparation at baccalaureate and graduate level—wide range of subjects supporting special education. Program funded through schools. For school list, write: Division of Personnel Preparation, Special Education Programs, Department of Education, Washington, DC 20202.

Travel
American Society of Travel Agents. Undergrad and graduate level, travel schools, junior college, CTC. U. S. or Canadian school. 3.0 GPA, 32 scholarships, $750-$1,200. Travel/tourism students. ASTA Scholarship Foundation, Inc., 1101 King Street, Alexandria, VA 22314. By June 10.

Vertical Flight
$2,000. Undergraduate and graduate. For career in vertical flight technology. Vertical Flight Foundation, 217 N. Washington St., Alexandria, VA 22314. By Feb. 1.

Chapter 22
Money for Minorities and Women

Many of you have a headstart, an edge, in the competition for need-based financial aid. Why? Because, statistically, the income of minority families is less than that of their majority contemporaries, and because the income of women is less than that of men who occupy equal positions. What these numbers say is that for once you have a leg up. You are a stride ahead. Take advantage of that lead.

Only after you have gone the traditional, need-based route, travelled it with savvy and in full control, should you look for the icing, found in this chapter.

Also, request a copy of *Higher Education Opportunities for Minorities and Women* from the Supt. of Documents, US Government Printing Office, Washington DC, 20402 ($4.25), and check Chapter 11 and all other chapters in Part VI.

In addition, nearly 25% of our nation's colleges and universities have special awards designed to encourage minority student enrollment. So what happened when the Department of Education recently proclaimed that schools awarding scholarships based on race were violating Federal civil rights law and would no longer be eligible for federal funds? The Administration's switchboard lit up (is this what Bush meant by A Thousand Points of Light?). The Department of Education wisely "rethought" the legality of minority-based scholarships and has encouraged schools to continue such making awards until it has a chance to review the situation further. The issue will probably wind up in the courts, but at least for now, awards are plentiful!

FEDERAL ASSISTANCE TO MINORITIES

All Minorities

Graduate Fellowship Program. Graduate study in science, mathematics, engineering. Master's level and doctorate. Up to three years of support. Approximately $12,300 per year. Write: Fellowship Office, National Research Council, 2101 Constitution Avenue, NW, Washington, DC 20418.

Legal Training for the Disadvantaged. $3 million program prepares students for entry into law school. Stipend. Also summer programs. Write CLEO, 1800 M St., NW, Suite 290, North Lobby, Washington, DC 20036.

Minority Access to Research Careers. Biomedical science. Funded through schools with substantial minority student bodies. Undergraduate (3rd year) through graduate level. For school list, write to MARC Program, National Institute of General Medical Sciences, National Institutes of Health, Westwood Bldg., Room 950, Bethesda, MD 20892.

Minority Participation in Graduate Education Programs. $6 million program to encourage minority students to pursue graduate education. Funded through 73 colleges. For school list write:Office of Higher Education Program Services, Department of Education, 400 Maryland Ave., SW, Washington DC, 20202

Native Americans

Native American Fellowship Program. Undergraduate programs in business, engineering, natural resources. Graduate programs in education, law, medicine, psychology, natural resources, business, engineering, clinical psychology. All tuition and stipends. Apply to Bureau of Indian Affairs, Scholarship Officer, Office of Indian Education Programs, MS-Room 3525, 1849 "C" St NW, Washington DC, 20242. By Jan. 1.

Indian Health Service Scholarships. Allied health fields to include pharmacy and nursing. Two programs: 1. Preparatory Scholarship Program. Two years. 2. Health Professions Scholarship Program. Both restricted to American Indian, Alaskan native. Tuition plus stipend. Also, a loan repayment program and extern (student) employment program. Apply to Indian Health Service, Twinbrook Plaza, Suite 100, 12300 Twinbrook Parkway, Rockville, MD 20852. By May 1.

Native American Scholarship Fund. Two programs. MESBEC and NALE Programs. (math, engineering, science, business, education, computers). The NALE Program allows native paraprofessionals in the schools to return to college and complete undergraduate degrees and/or teaching credentials. Students must be admitted or enrolled in college. Should have high grade point averages and high test scores. Contact 3620 Wyoming Blvd., N.E., Suite 206, Albuquerque, NM 87111. (505) 275-9788.

PRIVATE ASSISTANCE FOR MINORITIES

All Minorities

Accounting. Undergraduate and graduate for enrolled students. Approximately 400 awards. Individual grants up to $2,000. Apply by July 1 and December 1. Manager, Minority Recruitment, American Institute of Certified Public Accountants, 1211 Avenue of the Americas, New York, By 10036-8775.

Architecture. 20 awards, $500-$3,500. Renewable, up to 3 years. Nomination by guidance counselor, school, professional architect. Nomination deadline is Dec 1. For the top 2 - special $2,500 award, 4th, 5th, 6th year. Nomination forms from AIA, Scholarship Committee, 1735 New York Avenue, NW, Washington, DC 20006.

Dental Hygienists. For at least the second year of dental hygiene curriculum. To $1,500. Also $1,000 for student accepted into entry level dental hygiene program in cert. areas. American Dental Hygienists Assoc., Institute for Oral Health, Suite 3400, 444 N. Michigan, Chicago, IL 60611. By May 1.

Dentistry. 20-30 Scholarships of $1,000 for first year in dental school. By May 1 to American Fund for Dental Health, 211 East Chicago Ave., Suite 820, Chicago, IL 60611.

Engineering. $2 million plus awarded through schools. Schools select. Obtain scholarship guide and list of funded schools from National Action Council of Minorities in Engineering, 3 West 35th Street, New York, By 10001-2281.

Engineering. Tuition, fees, stipend of $5,000/academic year, travel to and from summer work site. US citizen. Carry full academic load towards a master's degree in engineering. Must intern at a member employer location during summer. National Consortium for Graduate Degrees for Minorities in Engineering, Executive Director, GEM Minorities Fellowships, Box 537, Notre Dame, IN 46556. 219-287-1097. By Dec. 1.

Engineering, Computer Science. AT&T ESP Scholarships. All expenses. 15 awards per year. By Jan 15 to AT&T Bell Laboratories, ATTN: ESP Admin., Crawfords Corner Road, Rm. 1E-213, Holmdel, NJ 07733-1988. (201) 949-3000 or (201) 949-4300 scholarships. Support application with three letters of recommendation from counselors, teachers, principal. Also Dual Degree Scholarship Program. 3 awards. Tuition, fees, books, living allowances, travel expenses, employment, etc. "B" or better. Contact Dual Degree Administrator, AT&T Bell Labs., Crawfords Corner Road, Rm. 1B-207, Holmdel, NJ 07733. By Jan. 15.

General Studies. Minority members of the United Methodist Church (for at least 1 year prior) Ethnic Scholarships, value: $100 to $1,000. By April 1 to Office of Loans & Scholarships, Board of Higher Education & Ministry, PO Box 871, Nashville, TN 37202.

General Studies. 1. Student Opportunity Scholarships for Communicant members of the Presbyterian Church, $100-$1,400. By April 1. 2. Native American Education Grant Program for Indians, Aleuts, and Eskimos pursuing post-secondary education. $200-$1,500. By June 1. Other scholarships, grants, loans. Manager, Financial Aid for Studies, Presbyterian Church, 100 Witherspoon St., Louisville, KY 40202-1396.

Geosciences. 35+ scholarships. Undergrad/grad. Undergrad up to $10,000/yr. Graduate to $4,000/yr. AGI-MPP, American Geological Institute, 4220 King St., Alexandria, VA 22302-1507. By Feb. 1.

Geosciences. Some information on private assistance for minorities in the geo sciences is also available from Lou Fernandez, Univ. of New Orleans, Lake Front, New Orleans, LA 70122.

Humanities. Tuition plus $9,000 stipend. Up to four years support leading to Ph.D. CIC Predoctoral Fellowships Program in Humanities, Kirkwood Hall 111, Indiana University, Bloomington, IN 47405. U. S. Citizen. By Jan.1.

Sciences. CIC Predoctoral Fellowships Program in the Sciences, Kirkwood Hall 111, Indiana University, Bloomington, IN 47405. By Jan.1. Will be funded through eligible institution.

Social Sciences. Tuition plus $9,000 stipend. Up to five years support leading to Ph.D. CIC Predoctoral Fellowships Program, Kirkwood 111, Indiana University, Bloomington, IN 47405. U.S. Citizen. By Jan.1.

Black

General Studies. HS senior. Scholarships up to $4,000. Academic achievement, leadership, financial need. Jackie Robinson Foundation, 80 Eighth Avenue, New York, By 10011, ATTN: Scholarship Program. April 15 deadline.

General Studies. National Achievement Scholarship Program for outstanding Negro Students. Enter the competition by taking PSAT/NMSQT. 350 non-renewable $2,000 scholarships, 375 renewable awards ($250-$8,000). Obtain Student Bulletin from National Merit Scholarship Corp., 1560 Sherman Avenue, Suite 200, Evanston, IL 60201.

Law. Accepted by law school. U.S. Citizen, LSAT, also awards for public interest law. Preferred consideration for need and under 35 years of age. Earl Warren Legal Training Program, 99 Hudson St., Suite 1600, New York, By 10013. By March 15.

Hispanic

General Studies. Ask for LULAC Center nearest you. SASE to LULAC National Scholarship Fund, 777 North Capitol St., N.E., Suite 305, Washington, DC 20002.

General Studies. Awards to enrolled undergraduate and graduate students with at least fifteen credit hours. Self-addressed stamped envelope to National Hispanic Scholarship Fund, ATTN: Selection Committee, POBox 728, Novata, CA 94948. Between June 5 and October 5.

General Studies. 500 $1,500 scholarships. By invitation only to students scoring high on the PSAT. Administered by College Board.

Law. 19 $1,000 scholarships and one $2,000 scholarship to students enrolled in law school. Also 3 special scholarships up to $2,000. Write: MALDEF, 634 S. Spring St., 11th Floor, Los Angeles, CA 90014. By May 30.

Native American

Graduate Study. $250-$10,000 Master's, doctorate and professional level assistance to needy students who are at least 1/4 American Indian or enrolled members of federally-recognized tribes. Write: American Indian Graduate Center, 4520 Montgomery Blvd., NE, Suite 1-B, Albuquerque, NM 87109. (505) 881-4584.

PRIVATE AID TO WOMEN

A tip to returning women: If you have small children who require care while you attend class, be sure to let the college know. Your student expense budget should then reflect the child care expense. The larger expense budget increases your need and will help you qualify for more aid.

Aerospace Engineering

$6,000 grants for graduate students. Women only. Zonta International Foundation, 557 W. Randolph St., Chicago, IL 60606. By December 31.

Athletics
Complete listing of colleges and universities offering athletic scholarships. Guide is available for $2.00 from Women's Sports Foundation, 342 Madison Ave., Suite 728, New York, 10173.

Banking and Business
Scholarships for members only. Write to National Association of Bank Women Scholarships, 500 North Michigan Ave., Suite 1400, Chicago, IL 60611.

Career
$3.5 million in local, state, and national awards. Apply early in junior year of high school. America's Young Woman of the Year Program Dept. DMO, PO Box 2786, Mobile, AL 36652. Awards count as taxable income.

Engineering
1. Society of Women Engineers. Approximately 38 scholarships, value from $500 to $3,000. Society of Women Engineers, United Engineering Center, Rm. 305, 345 East 47th Street, New York, By 10017.
2. Bell Labs Engineering. 15 Scholarships. All college costs. U. S. citizen. Recommendations from counselor, teachers, principal. AT&T Bell Laboratories, ATTN: ESP Admin., Crawfords Corner Road, Rm. 1E-213, Holmdel, NJ 07733-1988. Jan. 15 deadline.
3. BPW Loan Fund for Women in Engineering Studies. Loans. For further information and application forms, send a self-addressed business size envelope with 2 first class stamps to BPW Foundation, 2012 Massachusetts Avenue, NW, Washington, DC 20036.

General
Fellowships and grants for advanced research, graduate study, and community service. Female, U. S. citizen. Application by Nov. 15 for dissertation/postdoc. By Feb. 1 for research and project grants. American Assoc. of University Women, 2401 Virginia Ave., NW, Washington, DC 20037. (202) 728-7603.

Golf
1. Gloria Fecht Memorial Scholarship Fund. $1,500-$2,500 per year academic scholarships for qualified student golfers. California residents receive priority, then out-of-state applicants who will be attending a CA school. No specific level of golfing skill required. Applications due March 1. Gloria Fecht Memorial Scholarship Fund, 402 W. Arrow Hwy., Suite 10, San Dimas, CA 91773.
2. Women's Western Golf Foundation. Undergraduate scholarships. $8,000 ($2,000/yr.) toward room, board, tuition, fees. Interest in golf is important; golfing ability is not. Selected on basis of academic achievement, financial need, excellence of character. Contact Mrs. P. C. Marshall, 348 Granville Rd., Cedarburg, WI 53012. By April 1.

Older Women
1. Two programs. BPW Career Advancement and New York Life Foundation Scholarship for Women in the Health Professions. About 100 scholarships for mature women with critical financial need. Age over 30. Apply by April 15. For further information and application forms, send a self-addressed business size envelope with 2 first class stamps to Scholarship Department, BPW Foundation, 2012 Massachusetts Avenue, NW, Washington, DC 20036.
2. Training awards of $1,500 for women who want to upgrade their economic status through education. Sponsored by Soroptimists. Check your local telephone directory, Chamber of Commerce directory, or City Hall. By Dec. 15.

Pilots
Women pilots who wish to obtain helicopter rating. $4,000 awards. Apply by Nov 1 to Helicopter Association International, 1619 Duke St., Alexandria, VA 22314-3406.

Chapter 23
Special Situations:
The Non-Traditional Student

PHYSICALLY DISABLED

Physically disabled students frequently incur special expenses while attending college. Make sure these expenses are reflected in the student's budget (see Chapter 6). This, in turn, will increase your need and qualify you for more aid.

Your best source of information on special student aid is the Office of Vocational Rehabilitation in your state's education department.

For additional information, write: HEATH Resource Center, One Dupont Circle, NW, Suite 800, Washington, DC 20036-1193. 1-800-544-3284 or (202) 939-9320. HEATH stands for Higher Education & Adult Training for People with Handicaps.

Here are seven national programs that provide good work and some assistance:

- **The Alexander Graham Bell Association for the Deaf,** 3417 Volta Place, NW, Washington, DC 20007-2778, sponsors an annual scholarship awards program for profoundly deaf college students. $500 to $1,000. Apply by April 15.
- **American Council of the Blind** offers 15 scholarships ($1,000 to $2,000). April 1. Contact ACB, 1155 15th St. NW, Suite 720, Washington, DC 20005. 202-467-5081.
- **Council of Citizens With Low Vision** offers a one-year award of $1,000 for partially sighted undergraduate and graduate students. Applications must be typed. On or before April 1. Contact: National Office, CCLV, Riley Tower II, Suite 2300, 600 N. Alabama St., Indianapolis, IN 46204-1415. 1-800-733-2258 or (317) 638-8822.
- **National Association of the Deaf.** William C. Stokoe Scholarship, annual, $1,000. For deaf students pursuing part-time or full-time graduate studies in a field related to Sign Language, or the Deaf Community. Contact Stokoe Scholarship Secretary, National Association of the Deaf, 814 Thayer Avenue, Silver Spring, MD 20910. Deadline March 15.
- **Quota International Fellowship Fund.** (Fellowships). $1,000. 1420 21st Street, NW, Washington, DC 20036. (202) 331-9694. Deadline May 1.
- **Recording for the Blind.** Learning Through Listening Awards to HS seniors with specific learning disabilities who plan to continue their education. 3 awards, $2,000 each. By March 15. Contact: Lorraine Gresty, Recording for the Blind, 20 Roszel Road, Princeton, NJ 08540.
- **The Twitty, Milsap, Sterban Foundation.** Educational assistance to blind and visually impaired college and graduate students in all fields of study through partial scholarships. Enrolled in accredited college or graduate school program. Applications accepted from June 1-September 1. 600 Renaissance Center, Suite 1300, PO Box 43517, Detroit, MI 48243. (313) 567-1920.

PART-TIMERS

Most financial aid is based on being at least a half-time student. But take heart. The federal government's definition of "half-time" is more generous than that of most schools. Therefore, we urge you to apply for federal student aid (see Chapter 10). Under current law, colleges can set aside 10% of the SEOG and CW-S fund for assistance to part-time students.

Several states help part-time students. Check with your state (addresses in Chapter 11).

Our Suggestion: If at all possible, take an additional course, and boost your status to half-time.

ARE YOU 50, 60 OR OLDER?

If you plan to be at least a half-time student, you should remember that financial aid is awarded on the basis of need and not age. Hence, you can freely compete with those who are just out of high school and anybody else for all available financial aid.

If you plan to take just a few courses, you should know that many schools offer reduced tuition for older citizens. Many will even let you attend courses for free or on a space available basis. At least three states (Alabama, South Carolina and New Mexico) also offer reduced tuition for older citizens. Check your local college, your state higher ed office, or write to The Institute of Lifetime Learning, American Association for Retired Persons, 1909 K St. NW, Washington DC, 20049. Also, Adult Learning Services, The College Board, 45 Columbus Avenue, New York, NY 10023.

ARE YOU ONLY 25?

The National Association of Returning Students is a new association for the 7 million students over the age of 24. Write for information on their newsletter and list of resources. PO Box 3283, Salem OR 97302, 503-581-3731.

Chapter 24
A Few Words About Grad School

70% OF ALL GRADUATE AID

To learn where 70% of all graduate aid is, you will have to go back to the beginning of this book.

First, you must enhance your eligibility for aid. The lessons in Chapters 4 through 7 are as applicable to the graduate student as they are to the college-bound. The only thing different is the name of the financial aid application. Grad students must wrestle with a form that has the jawbreaker acronym of GAPSFAS.

Second, review Chapter 10 and become familiar with the major sources of aid available to you: the Stafford Loan, the SLS Loan for independent grad students, the Perkins Loan and College Work-Study. If your future is in a medical field, add Chapter 20 to your reading.

NOTE: Graduate students are not eligible for Pell Grants or SEOGs.

3% OF ALL GRADUATE AID

For 3% of all graduate aid, check Chapter 11. Alabama, Arizona, California, Colorado, Connecticut, Delaware, DC, Florida, Idaho, Iowa, Louisiana, Maryland, Massachusetts, Michigan, Mississippi, Nevada, New Hampshire, New Jersey, New Mexico, New York, North Carolina, Ohio, Oklahoma, Texas, Vermont, Virginia, and Puerto Rico offer some help to graduate students.

But be aware that many of these opportunities are sharply restricted in terms of major field of study (e.g., medicine) or population group which benefits (e.g., minority). Furthermore students must usually enroll in a school located in the state.

10% OF ALL GRADUATE AID

About 10% of all graduate aid is dispersed throughout this book. For instance, if you get a commission in the military and are willing to extend your period of service, you may qualify for graduate training.

The cooperative education route (Chapter 12) is rich in graduate opportunities. And you'll find more in Chapters 21 and 22.

12% OF ALL GRADUATE AID

For 12% of all graduate support you must talk to the department chairperson or dean at the school where you plan to pursue your graduate studies. Here is how these people can help you:
- With departmental scholarships and grants
- With graduate assistantships
- With internships and summer jobs
- With employment funded by a grant

Remember, in most instances, the professor gets the grant, but will need grad students to help count the chromosomes and wash out the test tubes.

1% OF ALL GRADUATE AID

That you have to discover yourself. Through research. The best bet starting points for research: two publications put out by the Foundation Center:
1. The current *Foundation Directory*.
2. The current *Foundation Grants to Individuals*.

We don't recommend you buy either reference. They are expensive. But do locate them in the reference room of the public library and spend some time looking through them.

You might also request *A Selected List of Fellowship Opportunities and Aids to Advanced Education* from The Publications Office, National Science Foundation, 1800 G Street, NW, Washington, DC 20550. This booklet contains information on fellowship opportunities for US citizens and foreign nationals in many fields of study (including the humanities, social sciences, engineering, physical sciences, math, and life/medical sciences). Undergraduate, graduate, post-doctoral.

4% OF ALL GRADUATE AID

Engineering and Science
Support of graduate education by the Department of Defense. Stipends and tuition. No service obligation. 1. Navy: ASEE, 11 DuPont Circle, Suite 200, Washington, DC 20036. (202) 745-3616. 2. Air Force: SCEEE, Fellowship Program, 1101 Massachusetts Ave., St. Cloud, FL 34769. 3. NDSEG Fellowship Program, 200 Park Drive, Suite 211, PO Box 13444, Research Triangle Park, NC 27709, Attn: Dr. George Outterson.

Engineering and Science
Fellowships. College seniors for graduate study. US citizenship required. Grad study at selected universities. GPA must be 3.0/4.0. Most on a work-study basis. Spend summer vacation working at Hughes Aircraft Co. Tuition, fees, stipend, travel and relocation expenses, salary for summer and other periods of full-time work. Hughes Aircraft Company, Technical Education Center, PO Box 45066, Bldg. C1/B168, Los Angeles, CA 90045-0066. (213) 568-6711.

Food and Agricultural Science
National Needs Graduate Fellows. Master's and doctor's level. Funded through school. For school list, write: US Office of Education, 400 Maryland Avenue, SW, Washington, DC 20202.

Graduate Fields
Graduate and Professional Study. Fellows pay no tuition or fees. $21 million program. (1) Patricia Roberts Harris Graduate Study Fellowships. Awards designed to increase participation of minorities and women who are underrepresented in academic/professional fields. (2) Patricia Roberts Harris Public Service Education Fellowships. Master's and doctorate level. Fellows selected by schools. Up to $10,000 stipend for 12 months for both programs. For school list, write: Graduate Programs Branch, Department of Education, 400 Maryland Avenue, SW, Washington, DC 20202-5251.

Humanities
Graduate study in the humanities. Tuition plus stipend. Approximately 80 awards. For information, write: Mellon Fellowships, Woodrow Wilson National Fellowship Foundation, PO Box 288, Princeton, NJ 08542.

Humanities, Arts, Social Sciences
Javits Fellowships. $8 million program. 125 fellowships of up to $16,000 per year. Contact: Graduate Programs Branch, Department of Education, 400 Maryland Avenue, SW, Washington, DC 20202.

International Business
Some student fellowships. 35 awards. Funded through schools. For school list, write: Office of International Studies Branch, Department of Education, Rm. 3054, ROB-3, 400 Maryland Avenue, SW, Washington, DC 20202.

International Exchange
Possession of B.A. degree. Live and study abroad as a Fulbright student. Write IIE, US Student Programs, 809 UN Plaza, New York, NY 10017. (212) 984-5330.

Languages and Teaching
Advanced language and area studies. Over 114 schools participate. Funded through schools. Schools select students. Tuition and stipends. For school list, write: Center for International Education (FLAS), US Dep. of Education, Washington, DC 20202-5331.

Librarianship
Library Career Training Program. Funded through schools. Schools select students. For list of schools, write: Library Development Staff, Library Programs, OERI, Department of Education, 555 New Jersey Avenue, NW, Washington, DC 20208-5571.

Marine Sciences
Marine Sciences. The National Sea Grant College Federal Fellows Program. Program funded by National Sea Grant College Program Office. For students who are in a graduate or professional degree program at an accredited institution of higher education. Request brochure from National Sea Grant College Program Office, Attn: Fellowship Director, 1335 East West Highway, Silver Spring, MD 20910.

Medical and Biological Sciences
Scholarships and Fellowships. Howard Hughes Medical Institute College seniors or first-year graduate students. Study leading to doctoral degrees in biological/medical sciences. 66 awards, consisting of $13,500 stipend plus $11,700 cost-of-education allowance to the fellowship institution. Renewable for up to five years. Office of Grants and Special Programs, Howard Hughes Medical Institute, 6701 Rockledge Drive, Bethesda, MD 20817. (301) 571-0526.

Music
The American Musicological Society offers 3 dissertation fellowships per year. Twelve-month stipend (non-renewable) of $10,000. Application forms from Secretary, AMS Fellowship Committee, Department of Music, New York University, 268 Waverly Building, Washington Square, New York, NY 10003. By October 1.

National Needs Areas
Stipends of $10,000 to enhance teaching and research in academic areas. These awards go to graduate students of superior ability who demonstrate financial need. $25 million program funded through 84 different schools. For listing, write Division of Higher Educational Incentive Programs, Office of Postsecondary Education, Department of Education, Rm. 3022, ROB-3, Mail Stop 3327, 7th & D Streets, SW, Washington, DC 20202.

Psychology
Two awards of $2,500 each for full-time doctoral students in psychology accepted into an accredited California school. By Oct. 15. California Psychological Association Foundation, 1010 11th Street, Suite 202, Sacramento, CA 95814. Students outside California might consider contacting their own state's affiliate of the American Psychological Association to inquire about scholarship assistance.

Science, Social Science, Math, Engineering

Graduate study in sciences, social sciences, mathematics and engineering. Three years of support. Approximately $12,300 per year. 750 new fellows yearly. Application from Fellowship Office, National Research Council, 2101 Constitution Avenue, NW, Washington, DC 20418. Request "Selected List of Fellowship Opportunities and Aids to Advanced Education," NSF 88-119 to Publications Office, 1800 G St., NW, Washington, DC 20550.

Space-Related Science and Engineering, Aerospace Research

Awards up to $22,000. Renewable. Graduate students. Also summer programs. For more information: Graduate Student Researchers Program, University Programs Branch, NASA Headquarters, Washington, DC 20546. Also, graduate and doctoral fellowships at affiliated schools. For more information: Space Grant College and Fellowship Program, University Programs Branch, NASA, Washington, DC, 20546.

IF ALL THIS DOESN'T COVER YOU

Investigate the commercial loan sources listed in Chapter 7. The combination of these loans and PLUS/SLS loans should be more than enough to cover education costs. In most instances, you have the option to defer payment while in school, and then take up to ten years to repay after deferment.

Chapter 25
A Treasure Chest of Tips

Students of the late seventies could always hope that if things were tight one year, the next year would be better, with more federal money flowing their way. Students today haven't been that lucky. They must cope with level aid funding while tuitions keep rising.

For these students, the slogan is "know more about every aspect of financial aid or dig deeper." To save you the purchase of a new shovel, here is a summary of the financial aid skills you, as a student today, must master.

1. Selecting a College (I). When picking a college, go beyond the normal search criteria, such as majors offered, academic reputation, size, and distance from home, and inquire about innovative tuition aid features. These may include matching scholarships, sibling scholarships, guaranteed cost plans, installment plans, special middle income assistance programs, tuition remission for high grades, acceleration opportunities, etc. See Chapter 9.
2. Selecting a College (II). All factors being equal, pick colleges most likely to offer you a financial aid package composed of grants and scholarships that don't have to be repaid. Such a package is a lot better than one made up of loans which will saddle you with a repayment burden for many years after graduation. Best bet: Any school in which your academic record places you in the upper 25% of the profile of the incoming freshman class. See Chapters 7 and 9.
3. Selecting a College (III). Always send applications to two colleges of equal merit. If you get accepted by both, you might be able to play one against the other in securing a more favorable package. See Chapters 7 and 9.
4. Try the External Degree Route. Here you win a sheepskin from an accredited school without ever leaving home or job. Such a diploma will cost less in money and time than if it had been earned through campus attendance. External degrees offer academic credit for documented learning and experience you have already acquired, and couples these with formal assessments. See Chapter 7.
5. Do Four Years Work in Three. There is no reduction in courses. You must attend summer school. But the compressed time will save you the "inflationary increase" of the fourth year of a regular program.
6. Spend Some Time at a Community College. Work hard. Get good grades. Transfer to a solid four-year institution. This way, you can pick up the halo of a prestige diploma at half the cost.
7. Understand How Need Analysis Works. By knowing the formulas, the shrewd parent or student can present the family financial picture in such a way as to obtain a more favorable need analysis. This isn't unlike the method used for presenting one's financial picture to the IRS so as to qualify for the smallest possible tax liability. See Chapters 6 and 7.
8. Try Some "What If?" Calculations. But first, learn how need analysis works. A typical "what if": Is this a good time for mom or dad to finish their college work, along with son and daughter? Or will it be more advantageous, financially, for your parent to go back to work and help with expenses? You'll be surprised at the dollar figures generated by "what if" drills. See Chapter 7.
9. Don't Pass Up the Entitlement Programs. Approximately $5 billion in low-interest, subsidized federal student loans go unused each year simply because students think they are ineligible, don't bother to go through the paper work hassle, or just don't know about the program. See Chapter 10 and College Loans From Uncle Sam.
10. Cash Flow (I). Search for a low-interest, private loan. Numerous states (Illinois, Massachusetts, Florida, Connecticut, Iowa, Pennsylvania, Maryland) have set up loan authorities

which float tax-exempt bonds to raise student loan money. And colleges themselves have received permission to issue such bonds. At the same time, private banks are becoming more innovative in sponsoring combination savings/lending plans. Keep an eye out for these developments. They can help middle-income families with the cash flow problem of paying for college. See Chapters 6, 7, and 9.

11. Cash Flow (II). Go to college on the house. Many home owners have accumulated large amounts of idle equity in their houses (equity is the difference between the home's value and the amount owed on the mortgage) and they want to put it to work. Your strategy: Releasing this equity either through a line of credit or through refinancing the first mortgage. See Chapters 7 and 9.

2. Negotiate With the Financial Aid Officer. The college financial aid officer will present you with a package of assistance that should, in theory, cover the difference between what college costs and what your family can contribute. If you feel the college really wants you, because you are a brain or an athlete or the child of an alumnus or can help with meeting a geographic or minority quota, you may want to negotiate the content of the package. Your objective: To increase the grant component (money that doesn't have to be repaid) and reduce the loan component (money you must repay). See Chapters 6, 7, and 9 and *Financial Aid Officers* (inside back cover).

13. Try for an Academic Scholarship. Over 1200 colleges offer academic scholarships to students with a B average and SAT scores of 900 or more. Middle income folks take notice: Most of these scholarships are not based on financial need. If you are just outside the SAT eligibility range for one of these awards, take a good SAT preparation course. It may raise your scores enough to enter the winner's circle. See Chapter 18 and *The A's and B's of Academic Scholarships* (inside back cover).

14. Go the Cooperative Education Route. Over 900 colleges offer cooperative education programs. Alternate formal study with periods of career-related work. Earn up to $7,000 per year during the work phase. It may take an extra year to win the degree, but it will be easier on the pocketbook. See Chapter 12 and *Earn & Learn* (inside back cover).

15. Athletic Student Aid. We aren't talking about the "Body by Nautilus, Mind by Mattel" tackle who can do 40 yards in 4 seconds. Nebraska will find that person. We're talking about students who are better than average in a variety of sports, ranging from tennis to golf to lacrosse. A great many colleges seek people who can be developed into varsity material. The rewards come in two forms: outright scholarships or an "improved" financial aid package. See Chapter 19.

16. Acceleration. Can you get credit for a semester or a year of college work? You can through the Advanced Placement Program or by enrolling in college courses in high school. When credits can cost as much as $250 each, receiving credit for a credit leaves money in the bank.

17. Be An Accurate, Early Bird. Be as accurate as possible in filling out financial aid forms. Submit them as early as you can. When resources are tight, it's first-come, first-served. Those who must resubmit their forms and those who are slow in applying come in at the end of the line. By then, all the money is gone. See Chapters 6 and 7.

18. Check the Military Offerings. Reserve enlistments are especially attractive. For a hitch in the National Guard you can pick up a state benefit, a federal bonus, partial loan forgiveness, drill pay, sergeant stripes (if you also participate in ROTC), and in some cases, tuition remission at the state university. And these are not either/or opportunities. You can have most of them, or all of them. See Chapter 13.

19. Take Advantage of Teacher Mania. Individual colleges, most states, and Uncle Sam all have loan forgiveness programs for prospective teachers. Go this route and your education will cost you very little. You teach Ohm's law for four years to pay off the obligation. You pick up a little maturity, a lot of patience. You contribute to the well-being of hundreds of scholars-to-be. And you're still young enough to begin a different career if teaching is not for you. Chapters 9 and 11.

20. Sacrifice. You may have to give up a few luxuries: Cancelling your pet's Beverly Hills grooming sessions can save you $3,200 per dog per year; using a Volkswagen instead of your Lear jet can save you $540 per tank of gas.

Appendices

Appendix 1
FAMILY CONTRIBUTION FOR DEPENDENT STUDENTS (1992/93 ACADEMIC YEAR)

PARENTS' CONTRIBUTION FROM INCOME
1. Parents' Adjusted Gross Income .... $ _____
2. Parents' Untaxed Social Security Benefits .... $ _____
3. Parents' Aid to Families With Dependent Children Benefits. ..... $ _____
4. Parents' Other Nontaxable Income. This may include child support received, unemployment compensation, workman's compensation, disability payments, interest on tax-exempt bonds, housing, food and living allowances for military, clergy or others... $ _____
5. IRA, KEOGH and 401(k) payments made by parents. .... $ _____
6. **Total Income.** Add Lines 1 through 5. .... $ _____
7. US Income Taxes paid. .... $ _____
8. State Income Taxes paid .... $ _____
9. Social Security Taxes paid. .... $ _____
10. Family Maintenance Allowance from Table A. .... $ _____
11. Employment Expense Allowance. If both parents work, enter 35% of the lower income or $2,500, whichever is less. If your family has a single head of household who works, enter 35% of that income or $2,500, whichever is less. .... $ _____
*12. Unreimbursed Medical and Dental Expenses that exceed 5% of Line 6. .... $ _____
*13. Elementary and Secondary School Tuitions paid to a maximum of $4,639 per student. .... $ _____
14. **Total Allowances.** Add Lines 7 through 13. .... $ _____
15. **Parents' Available Income.** Line 6 minus Line 14. .... $ _____

PARENTS' CONTRIBUTION FROM ASSETS
*16. Cash and Bank Accounts. .... $ _____
*17. Home Equity (Market value of home less what is owed on it). .... $ _____
*18. Other Real estate, investments, stocks, bonds, trust funds, commodities, precious metals. .... $ _____
*19. Business and/or Farm Net Worth from Table B. .... $ _____
*20. **Total Assets.** Add Lines 16 through 19. .... $ _____
*21. Asset Protection Allowance. From Table C. .... $ _____
*22. Discretionary Net Worth. Line 20 minus Line 21. .... $ _____
*23. **CONTRIBUTION FROM ASSETS.** Multiply Line 22 by the percentage from Table D. This may be a negative value. .... $ _____

PARENTAL CONTRIBUTION
24. Adjusted Available Income. Add Lines 15 and 23. .... $ _____
25. **PARENT CONTRIBUTION.** From Table E. If negative, enter 0. .. $ _____
26. Number in College Adjustment. Divide Line 25 by the number in college (at least half-time) at the same time. Quotient is the contribution for each student. .... $ _____

STUDENT'S CONTRIBUTION FROM INCOME

27. Student's Adjusted Gross Income. .... $ _____
28. Untaxed Social Security Benefits .... $ _____
29. Other Untaxed income and benefits. .... $ _____
30. Total Income. Add lines 27, 28, and 29. .... $ _____
31. US Income Taxes paid. .... $ _____
32. State Income Taxes paid. .... $ _____
33. Social Security Taxes paid. .... $ _____
34. Total Allowances. Add Lines 31 through 33. .... $ _____
35. Students Available Income. Line 30 minus Line 34. .... $ _____
36. **STUDENT'S CONTRIBUTION FROM INCOME.**
    Multiply Line 35 by 70%. If the result is less than $700 (for first year undergraduates) or $900 (for any other student), use $700 or $900 instead. .... $ _____

STUDENT'S CONTRIBUTION FROM ASSETS

*37. Add all of student's assets—cash, savings, trusts, investments, real estate. .... $ _____
*38. **STUDENT'S CONTRIBUTION FROM ASSETS.** Take 35% of Line 37. .... $ _____

FAMILY CONTRIBUTION

39. If one student is in college, add lines 25, 36, and 38. .... $ _____
40. If two or more students are in college at the same time, add for each, Lines 26, 36, and 38. .... $ _____

If either parent is a dislocated worker, use expected 1992 income (taxable and nontaxable) for Lines 1 through 5, and Line 11. Use 1991 tax tables to estimate taxes paid for Lines 7, 8, and 9. Home equity (line 17) will be $0. Home equity will also be $0 if either parent is a displaced homemaker.

*If you qualify for the simplified formula, the starred items will all equal $0. Dislocated workers who opt to use the simplified formula must use previous year (1991) income.

Appendix 2
FAMILY CONTRIBUTION FOR INDEPENDENT STUDENTS WITH DEPENDENTS (1992/93 ACADEMIC YEAR)

CONTRIBUTION FROM INCOME

1. Student's (and Spouse's) Adjusted Gross Income. .... $ _____
2. Student's (and Spouse's) Social Security Benefits .... $ _____
3. Student's (and Spouse's) Aid to Families With Dependent Children Benefits. .... $ _____
4. Student's (and Spouse's) Other Nontaxable Income. This may include child support received, unemployment compensation, workman's compensation, disability payments, interest on tax-exempt bonds, housing, food and living allowances for military, clergy or others. .... $ _____
5. IRA, KEOGH, 401 (k) Payments made by Student (and Spouse). .... $ _____
6. **Total Income.** Add Lines 1 through 5. .... $ _____
7. US Income Taxes paid. .... $ _____

8.	State Income Taxes paid.	$ _____
9.	Social Security Taxes paid.	$ _____
10.	Family Maintenance Allowance from Table A.	$ _____
11.	Employment Expense Allowance. If both student and spouse work, enter 35% of the lower income or $2,500, whichever is less; If student qualifies as head of household, enter 35% of income or $2,500, whichever is less.	$ _____
*12.	Unreimbursed Medical and Dental Expenses that exceed 5% of Line 1.	$ _____
*13.	Elementary and Secondary School Tuitions paid to a maximum of $4,639 per student.	$ _____
14.	**Total Allowances.** Add Lines 7 through 13.	$ _____
15.	**Available Income.** Line 6 minus Line 14. If the result is less than $700 (for first year undergraduates) or $900 (for any other student), use $700 or $900 instead.	$ _____
*16.	VA benefits that will be received during the 92/93 academic year (include GI Bill and VEAP benefits).	$ _____

CONTRIBUTION FROM ASSETS (Combine Student's and Spouse's Assets)

*17.	Cash and Bank Accounts.	$ _____
*18.	Home Equity (Market value of home less what is owed on it).	$ _____
*19.	Other Real estate, investments, stocks, bonds, trust funds, commodities, precious metals.	$ _____
*20.	Business and/or Farm Net Worth from Table B.	$ _____
*21.	**Total Assets.** Add Lines 17 through 20.	$ _____
*22.	Asset Protection Allowance. From Table F.	$ _____
*23.	Discretionary Net Worth. Line 21 minus Line 22.	$ _____
*24.	**CONTRIBUTION FROM ASSETS.** Multiply Line 23 by percentage from Table D. This may be a negative value.	$ _____
25.	Adjusted Available Income. Add Line 15, Line 16, and Line 24.	$ _____
26.	**TOTAL CONTRIBUTION.** From Table E.	$ _____
27.	Number in College Adjustment. Divide Line 26 by the number in college (at least half-time) at the same time. Quotient is the contribution for each student.	$ _____

If either the student or spouse is a dislocated worker, use expected 1992 income (taxable and nontaxable) for each in lines 1 through 5. Use 1991 tax tables to estimate taxes paid for lines 7,8, and 9. Home equity (line 18) will be $0. Home equity will also be $0 if the student (or spouse) is a displaced homemaker.

*If you qualify for the simplified formula, the starred items will all equal $0. Dislocated workers who opt to use the simplified formula must use previous year (1991) income.

Appendix 3
FAMILY CONTRIBUTION FOR INDEPENDENT STUDENTS WITHOUT DEPENDENTS (1992/93 ACADEMIC YEAR)

CONTRIBUTION FROM INCOME

1.	Student's Adjusted Gross Income.	$ _____
2.	US Income Taxes paid.	$ _____
3.	State Income Taxes paid.	$ _____
4.	Social Security Taxes paid.	$ _____
5.	Maintenance Allowance of $600 per month during periods of non-enrollment.	$ _____

6. Total Allowances. Add Lines 2 through 5. .... $ _____
7. **Available Income.** Line 1 minus Line 6. .... $ _____
8. Contribution From Available Income. If Line 7 is less than $10,600, take 70% of Line 7. If Line 7 is greater than or equal to $10,600, take $7,420 plus 90% of the amount greater than $10,600. $ _____
*9. VA Benefits that will be received during the 92/93 academic year (include GI Bill and VEAP benefits). .... $ _____
10. Untaxed Social Security Benefits. .... $ _____
11. Other Non-taxable Benefits (see Lines 3 and 4 of Appendix 1 for List). .... $ _____
12. **Contribution from Income.** Line 8 plus Lines 9 through 11. .... $ _____
13. If Line 12 is less than $1200, use $1200 instead. .... $ _____

CONTRIBUTION FROM ASSETS

*14. Cash and Bank Accounts. .... $ _____
*15. Home Equity (Market value of home less what is owed on it). .... $ _____
*16. Other Real estate, investments, stocks, bonds, trust funds, commodities, precious metals. .... $ _____
*17. Business and/or Farm Net Worth from Table B. .... $ _____
*18. **Total Assets.** Add Lines 14 through 17. .... $ _____
*19. Asset Protection Allowance. From Table F. .... $ _____
*20. Discretionary Net Worth. Line 18 minus Line 19. .... $ _____
*21. **CONTRIBUTION FROM ASSETS.** Multiply Line 20 by 35%. If negative, adjust to 0. .... $ _____
22. **TOTAL CONTRIBUTION. Add Line 12 or 13 and Line 21.** .... $ _____

If the student is a dislocated worker, use expected 1992 income (taxable and nontaxable) in lines 1,9,10, and 11. Use 1991 tax tables to estimate taxes paid for lines 2,3, and 4. Home equity (Line 15) will be $0. Home equity will also be $0 if the student is a displaced homemaker.

*If you qualify for the simplified formula, the starred items will all equal $0. Dislocated workers who opt to use the simplified formula must use previous year (1991) income.